DESIGNS
AND OTHER VERSES

DESIGNS

AND OTHER VERSES

BY
PAUL ADER

THE PENTLAND PRESS

EDINBURGH · CAMBRIDGE · DURHAM

First published in 1992 by
The Pentland Press Ltd.
Brockerscliffe
Witton-le-Wear
Durham

ISBN 1 872792 38 2

Typesetting by
Print Origination (NW) Ltd.,
Stephenson Way, Formby, Liverpool
Printed and bound in Britain by
Antony Rowe Ltd, Chippenham, Wiltshire
Jacket design by Geoff Hobbs

These Verses Be
Dedicated to
Cicely

Mi Casa Es Su Casa

Other Books by Paul Ader

We Always Come Back, 1945, W. H. Allen Co. Ltd., London

The Leaf Against the Sky, 1947, Crown Publishers, New York

How to Make a Million at the Track, 1977, Henry Regnery Company, Chicago

The Big Win, 1984, Pentland Press Ltd., Edinburgh, Scotland

The Commander, 1985, Pentland Press Ltd., Edinburgh, Scotland

Acknowledgements

Permission has been granted for the following quotations and references from the book, *A Brief History Of Time*, by Stephen Hawking, published by Bantam Doubleday Dell, 1988 Edition:

Page 70. 'Real gravitons make up what classical physicists call gravitational waves, which are very weak — and so difficult to detect that they have never yet been observed.'

Page 73: 'In this book I have given special prominence to the laws that govern gravity, because it is gravity that shapes the large-scale structure of the universe, even though it is the weakest of the four categories of forces.'

Pages 81–82: '. . . a star that was sufficiently massive and compact would have such a strong gravitational field that light could not escape . . . .'

Table of Contents

Helpful Hints on How to Write Verses   1
The Genesis and Evolution of a Poem   11

PART I   PROLOGUE

A Book For All Seasons   17
A List Of What I Think I Am   18
A Photograph   19
The Artist   20
Bad Poets Plagiarize   21
The Brook Sings Its Melody   22
Come, Cicely, Let Us See   23
The Creative Mind   24
Designs   25
Harvest   26
I Am Hard To Satisfy   27
If The Color Means   28
If You Tell Me Why   29
In Praise Of Plagiarism   30
Mi Casa Es Su Casa   31
Morning, Noon And Eventide   32
Reluctant Night   33
Some Say   34
Somewhere   35
Spending   36
Surprise   37
Tell Me   38
Things That Truly I Deplore   39
Two Little Girls   40

PART II NATURE

A List Of Things That Birds Do 43
As 44
At Sundown 46
Color Is The Key 47
Day 48
The Desert 49
Fearful Nature 53
Gravity 54
It Is Time 55
Like 56
Like The First 57
The Months Of Spring 58
The Moon 59
Nature 60
Nature's Irregularities 61
Nature's Law 63
Never As 64
Perhaps 65
Rain 66
Russian Evening 67
The Seasons 68
Shade Trees 69
Shadows 70
The Silent Seasons 71
The Sun 72
Sun, Moon And Stars 74
Sun, Moon And Stars – 2 75
Sun, Moon And Stars – 3 76
Thunder And Lightning 77
Trees 78
The Vagaries Of Nature 79
When 80
When The Trees Put On Their Joseph Coats 81
Wide As A Dream 82
Wind And Water 83
The Wind 84
The Wind – 2 85
The Winds Of Spring 86

PART III TRAVEL

A List Of Places I Have Never Been, But Maybe You Have   89
Carlsbad Caverns   90
China Is Dark   92
The City at Night   93
El Niño   94
English Journey   95
Glacier National Park   98
Grand Canyon   99
Iowa   100
Journeys   101
On the Way To Sante Fe   102
Petrified Forest   103
Redwoods   104
Yosemite   105

PART IV   MORALS AND METAPHYSICS

The ABC's   109
A Haunting Dream That Lingered   110
All   111
A List Of Things Hard To Believe   112
A List Of Things That Slip Away   113
A Man Is More   114
Apathy   115
Appearances   116
Artifice   117
A Single   118
Aspects Of Childhood   119
Awkward   120
Beauty   121
Betrayal   122
Beware   123
Body Language   124
Chaos   125
Coincidence   128
Consensus   129
Curiosity   130
Declarations   131

Design   132
Details   133
Did You Know? And Can You Tell Me Why?   134
Does?   136
Dreams   137
The Fallacy Of Logic   138
Fear   139
Fictionized   140
Fortune   141
The Future   142
Gambling   143
The Great Magician   144
Greed   145
Happiness   146
Happiness Is Just Around the Corner   147
Heaven And Hell   148
History   151
Home   152
Hormones   153
Hostage   154
I Don't Know   155
If   156
I Must Not   157
In Defense Of Darwin   158
Inspiration   160
I Offer No Apology   161
It Cannot Be Learned   162
The Judgment Day   163
Just How Much Does An Oak Tree Know?   164
Laughter   165
Laughter - 2   166
Life   167
Lighter Than A Breath   168
Lost in the Computer   169
Love   170
A Miracle   171
Miracles   172
Moderation   173
The Moment When   174

Money	175
More	176
Mystery	177
New ABCs	178
The New Reality	179
Niche Is In	180
Now, Go, My Love	181
Not Too Greedy	182
One With The Other	183
Order	184
Out Of Reach	185
Paradoxes	186
Paradoxes - 2	187
The Paradox Of Vanity	188
The Passing Of Remoteness	189
People	190
Pleasure	191
Power	192
Problems	193
Prosperity	194
The Question Of Ownership	195
Reality	197
Remembered	198
Riches, Fame And Pleasure	199
Say What You Will	201
Seeds	202
Silence	203
Statistics	205
Tension	206
Things That Count	207
Think Your Way	208
Thoughts	209
Three Things Most Needed Are	210
Time	211
The Tree Of Life	212
Truth	214
Truth And Error	215
Truth And Fiction	217
Truth Is No Stranger	219

Uniqueness   220
Variety   221
War   222
What Care I?   223
What Do You Do?   224
What If By Chance?   226
Why?   227
Why, Oh, Why?   228
Windows   229
Wit   230
Wonder   231
Words To The Wise   232

PART V   MISCELLANY
A Gemstone Calendar   235
A List Of People I Have Never Known, But Maybe You Have   238
A List Of Things That Are Blue   239
A List Of Things That Are Soft   240
A List Of Things That Catch The Light   241
A Toast   242
Braces   243
Coffee   245
Cowboys   246
The Dow   248
Garage Sales   249
Horse Racing   250
Lite   251
Memos   252
One More   253
Stolen   254
Stretching   255
The Nightly News   256
Too   257
Universal Questions   259
The Urban Hum   261
To Verbal-ize   262
Yawning   264

NOTES   267
ABOUT THE AUTHOR   289

Helpful Hints on
How to Write Verses

LET IT BE KNOWN to all here present that the book you hold in your hands is a book of verses, not a book of poems. There is a very considerable difference between verses and poems. It takes a poet to write poems, and I am not a poet. Fiction is my realm; four novels have preceded this volume. Words and symbols are the building blocks of fiction and poetry, but the true poet possesses a frenzy that is as rare as it is remarkable. The poet sculpts his lines from words and symbols just as nature sculpts the storm from clouds and sky.

Words flow from the poet's pen like sparkling spring water into a lake. Images are the wind beneath a poet's wings. In his introduction to *Lyrical Ballads*, Wordsworth said, 'Poetry is the breath and finer spirit of all knowledge; it is the impassioned expression which is the countenance of all Science.'

'Poetry,' wrote Matthew Arnold, 'is simply the most beautiful, impressive and . . . effective mode of saying things.'

Robert Frost comes closer to the dynamic truth: 'Poetry is a way of taking life by the throat.'

According to Shelley, 'Poetry is the record of the best and happiest moments of the happiest and best minds.'

Writing on Shakespeare, Coleridge declared that, 'Prose is words in the best order; poetry is the *best* words in their *best* order.' But Coleridge and Shelley, in these statements, do not emphasize that most necessary element, *passion*. The poet is an artist, and the artist must have a high degree of passion.

Edgar Allan Poe affirmed that, 'With me poetry has been not a purpose but a passion, and the passion should be held in reverence.'

Once again, I affirm that I am *not* a poet. The true poet has talent, yes, but much more. William Blake wrote, 'Poetry, painting and music are the three powers in man conversing with Paradise.'

On the other hand, every composition by a true poet is not a poem. I would estimate that the majority of those compositions fall back into the category of verses. Still, the writer of verses must have talent and dedication and persistence. To compose a series of verses that are worthy of publication is no small accomplishment. Most of the short verses herein originated from ideas gleaned from my reading, or from personal experiences, from my observations of people and nature. The close and intense observation of nature will provide subjects, ideas and images needed for the writing of poetry – or verse.

Travel about the world is also a good source of subjects. I have traversed much of the United States, England and Scotland. During my military career, I was stationed in England for six years, 1943–1945 in World War II, and 1960–1964 at R.A.F. Chicksands, located ten miles from Bedford, forty miles from London and thirty miles from Cambridge. Several of my 'poems' come out of these years of my stay in the British Isles.

My wife and I have travelled the northwestern United States. My wife grew up in Seattle and graduated from Lincoln High School. My sister, Mary Bonkemeyer, lived in San Miguel de Allende, Mexico, where she taught a course in art, and where she took a course in poetry writing. This was in 1976–1977, and her instructor was the poet Tom O'Grady. To get the students started, they were to make a list of subjects, of words and phrases. Mary made her lists, observing that several of them especially intrigued her – such as the words 'pigeons' and 'peach pits' and 'pots' for whatever use. She wrote a poem which she titled 'A List of Things Hard to Hold'. When my wife and I were visiting her in Santa Fe, she presented me with the following composition:

A List of Things Hard to Hold

By Mary Bonkemeyer

Peach pits,
Pigeons,
Diamonds,
And tickets to Disney World, and breath.

A pot for rainbows,
A fist,
Egypt's sands,
Hot coals, and the line.

Butterflies,
Tigers,
Dimes and quarters,
Lovers by two, and salty tears.

The idea of creating a composition from a List intrigued me, and I wrote half-a-dozen or so such poems, which are scattered throughout this volume.

Ideas, images, similes, metaphors – they're everywhere. I glean them from my wide reading, from my travels, my personal and professional experiences. When I read, I have beside me pen and paper. I jot down the more descriptive words and phrases, whatever catches my fancy. I favor magazines such as *The Atlantic* and *The New Yorker*. I dip into the novels of John Updike, the short stories of Alice Munroe, the mystery tales of P. D. James. Ms James, by the way, is more than a writer of mysteries. She is an accomplished novelist, with an astonishing knowledge of human personality.

Of course, I do not use *all* of the words and phrases I come across in my reading. Most of them never appear again. The point is that one must read, read, read, if one is to write, write, write. Those six words are the important words in the formula for successful creative composition. Saturate yourself in the literature of the past and the present. After a period of incubation, there appears the light of illumination, and a poem is born. The same is true of any practioner of the arts, as well as those in the field of science. Each of the arts has a long tradition behind it. Poems and verses arise from the ashes of the past. Truly, there is nothing *new* under the sun. Each generation must create its own version of history, of experience, of art, of science, of whatever.

Poems and verses appear on the page, and their arrangement is a matter of importance. Both the eye and the ear are involved in the understanding and appreciation of the words. My concern at the moment is with the eye, with the way the words are set down, the patterns they fall into. A book of poems or verses should have variety in good measure. Lines and stanzas should live and leap and tumble about on every page. Perhaps I have gone a bit overboard in my search for variety. As you read through the volume, you will note the wide variation in word and line arrangement. Here is but one brief example of the kind of arrangement I seem to favor, from the poem called 'Harvest'.

> Beauty is
> 'The harvest of a quiet eye.'
> A poem is
> To hold that harvest high.

'The harvest of a quiet eye' comes from Stanza 13 of Wordsworth's poem, 'A Slumber Did My Spirit Seal' (1799). I supplied the opening words, 'Beauty is . . . ' and added the two final lines. As you will note, I placed that segment at the end of the composition, a sort of climax to the poem.

A more extreme use of word arrangement occurs in the verse on 'Wit':

> If
> Brevity
> Is
> The
> Soul
> Of
> Wit,
> This is it!

'Brevity is the soul of wit,' was spoken by Hamlet, Act 2, Scene 2, Line 90.

Speaking generally, however, my verses are traditionally arranged, with only slight variations of line and stanza. There is a danger of being too clever in these matters. Remember e.e. cummings? I have consciously allowed myself to utilize the common variations of line and stanza. The first four lines of 'People':

> People say that people are
> Creation's oddest creatures.
> People say that people have
> The very oddest features.

A modest variation occurs in 'I Offer No Apology':

> I offer no apology
> When I present
> The long and short of hi-technology,
> When I accent
> The hard and soft of plant biology.

The two stanzas above also illustrate the use of rhyme. Poems need not rhyme, and many do not. But the ear delights in the harmony of sounds.

Children are natural artists, almost from birth, and many of them retain their natural talent into adulthood. And children love rhyme.

> Jack and Jill went up the hill
> To fetch a pail of water;
> Jack fell down and broke his crown,
> And Jill came tumbling after.

From *The Oxford Dictionary Of Nursery Rhymes*

Internal rhyme and penultimate-syllable rhymes are common in nursery poems. For an example of the latter, see above: 'creatures' and 'features'. Rhyme is one of the most frequently used tools in humorous verse, as practised by Ogden Nash, Phyllis McGinley, *et al*. Rhyme is not a hit-or-miss sort of thing. But it has almost infinite variations. Rhyme schemes are often *abab*, or *abba*, or more complex arrangements, as in sonnets. In my verses on 'Lists', I rhyme the last line of the stanzas. In my composition 'Fear,' I use six-line stanzas with a different rhyme arrangement, *aab*, *ccb*, in which *a* and *c* are repeat rhymes. Here's the final stanza:

> I feared to ask where space ends,
> For fear that space ends

Here.
I feared to ask what life means,
For fear that life means
Fear.

In the above, the recurrence of the 'fear' sound is also a kind of rhyme. Of course, the verses express an idea which is unusual and which may strike some people as nonsense. As in many poems or verses, *nonsense* is itself a tool which writers use. Lewis Carroll is the king in this kingdom:

And, as in uffish thought he stood,
  The Jabberwock, with eyes of flame,
Came whiffling through the tulgey wood,
  And burbled as it came!

From *Alice Through the Looking-Glass* (1872)

I confess I haven't done much 'burbling' in these verses, but I have a weakness for paradox and mystery. Here's a short excerpt from 'Paradoxes'.

Stupid is a twin to clever,
Joining often means to sever,
The instant is forever.

And here's the first stanza of 'Mystery'.

Beauty wears mystery's clothes,
Whisps of silk whisper secrets,
Hat and gloves carry codes
That have yet to be broken.

Next, a stanza from 'Think Your Way'.

The path to truth,
We learn from history,
Like every other thing,
Is veiled in mystery.

These verses begin with an 'idea' and express a conviction of mine that reason is a valuable tool but cannot be depended upon for the final word on anything in the universe. Indeed, there *is no final word*! All life is in the process of becoming and continuing *ad infinitum*.

More often than not, poems and verses have a certain cadence, a beat which we recognize and delight in. There is music in good poetry, and I truly wish that I possessed the talent. In a few of my compositions, the lines seem to sing, like the brook in 'The Brook Sings Its Melody'.

> The brook sings its melody
> To the coming night,
> The birds lift their colloquy
> To the dawning light.

In my composition on 'If The Color Means', I have attempted to infuse a bit of music:

> If blue means fidelity,
> Then I am blue for you.
> If yellow means maturity,
> Then I am yellow, too.

Another beat is apparent in 'Two Little Girls'.

> Two little girls
> In a meadow playing,
> One in pink,
> Blue the other.

> Two little girls
> By the brook a-straying,
> One is sister
> To the other.

In 'English Journey' these two lines:

> Blowing clouds scud the sky,
> Willows weep along the Cam.

Alliteration is the key to the lilt. In the first line, the 's' sound recurs, and in the second line it's the 'w' sound. If you've been to Cambridge and visited the Colleges, you can see, in your mind's eye, the willows weeping along the river Cam.

But closer to home, that is, in San Antonio, Texas, where more than half the population is Hispanic, the final stanza of '*Mi Casa Es Su Casa*' is a little song.

> *Mi casa es su casa,*
>   My house upon the hill,
> *Mi casa es su casa,*
>   If come you only will.

Poets love alliteration, just as they love 'simile' and 'metaphor'. It's a simile when one thing is 'like' another. It's metaphor when one thing *is* another. There are a dozen illustrations of both in the verses that follow. I shall only illustrate briefly. Here is 'simile' at work, from 'Iowa'.

> Sun, like silver,
> Coats the clouds after storm.
> Barns, like churches,
> Watch over aisles of corn.

In 'Love', the word 'like' appears fourteen times, which means there must be fourteen similes in the composition. Ordinarily, of course, the poet or versifier uses 'similes' selectively. Otherwise, they tend to lose their effectiveness.

Metaphors are a favorite writing tool, especially among poets. In my composition. 'Life', several metaphors occur in the final stanza:

> Love
> Is a tree growing in a garden.
> 'A garden
> Is a river running south.'
> South
> Is life without a warden.
> Life
> Is a city at the river's mouth.

A metaphor and a simile are sometimes used together. In my composition, 'As', I use this combination frequently.

> The wind is a seamless sheet,
> Clear as a bell.
> . . . .
> The universe is a cosmic swimming hole,
> Deep as a well.

James J. Kilpatrick, an expert in the field of the writer's art, notes: 'Good similes must be brief . . . and must stay in pitch. Good similes must also be original . . . . The same guidelines that apply to similes apply also to metaphors. They have to be consistent . . . original . . . and kept tightly in hand . . . . Metaphors are rope bridges over deep chasms. One slip and there we go.'

There are some who call themselves poets who delight in reverse similes or reverse images. I plead guilty, with this: 'The sky at noon/Is as blue as a Buick.' When nature is assigned human characteristics, that, too, is reverse imagery. Once again, I'm guilty.

> The sun at time of setting
> Is more beautiful than most –
> Colors rampant in a field
> To which the sky is host.

The artist and the poet are kin beneath the skin. The interchange of images is frequent. I use 'light' to bring the two together:

> The vagaries of nature
> Are in paintings most pronounced,
> Watch the ways that rays of light
> Wrap an object round about.

In the two final lines, alliteration is used to crown the effect. Robert Hughes, who writes about Art in *Time* magazine, pointed out that artists use rays of light 'to wrap an object' round about. The two stanzas quoted above are from my composition, 'The Vagaries Of Nature'. From that same poem, there is a good example of simile:

> The moon casts its shadows
> Like a many-fingered ghost.

There is a very close relationship among nature, art and poetry. In an examination of the works of the Lake Country Poets – Wordsworth and Coleridge – one can find a hundred, indeed, a thousand illustrations of this point. One example will suffice. In his famous 'Lines Composed A Few Miles Above Tintern Abbey,' Wordsworth writes:

> The sounding cataract
> Haunted me like a passion; the tall rock
> The mountain, and the deep and gloomy wood,

Their colours and their forms, were then to me
An appetite; a feeling and a love,
That had no need of a remoter charm,
By thoughts supplied, nor any interest
Unborrowed from the eye.

Like the beggar, the poet lives 'in the eye of nature'. But, unlike the beggar, only the poet, in his heart, feels 'The witchery of the soft sky!'

It is the poet, observing the fruits of nature's bounty, who converts reality into art by 'The harvest of a quiet eye'. Writing of the Daisy, Wordsworth says, 'Oft on the dappled turf at ease/ I sit, and play with similes'. The poet's subjects were 'meadow, grove, and stream,/The earth and every common sight,' which, bathed in the 'celestial light' of the poet's mind and heart, became little works of art.

I, of course, am not a poet, and you will find herein but a small harvest, and yet I can't deny that, on occasion, my mind has seen that celestial light, and my heart has trembled with the passion of the poet. Talent, and the ability to write, are things of mystery. Some say that it is in the genes. It's a matter of inheritance. Others contend that a poet is not born but is 'made'. I'm not the one to solve that puzzle, so I shall not try.

The Genesis and Evolution of a Poem

It may be of help – or, at least, of interest – to some of my readers if I describe the genesis and evolution of one composition, 'Truth Is No Stranger'. The British novelist, P. D. James, capped her literary career when, in 1989, she wrote *Devices And Desires*. As I mentioned earlier, I read with pen and paper by my side. One of the many quotes I noted down was, 'Truth is no stranger to improbability.'

The idea interested me by reason of the element of paradox. I had already composed half a dozen or more 'poems' on 'Truth' and 'Paradoxes'. I suspect that paradoxes come into play when the mind is unable to establish those subtle connections that exist everywhere. I believe that 'coincidences' don't really exist. If the mind could penetrate deep enough and see far enough, the 'connections' would become obvious. Coincidences are the children of ignorance.

Similarly, a paradox is just 'apparent'. It seems to be so. 'Truth is no stranger to improbability'. A thing may be true even though it appears to be improbable. Reality contains a goodly portion of illusion. Reality doesn't exist; it is created by the logical mind at work. The random and the chaotic are the natural state of affairs. The scientist and the observer of nature put together the realities that are useful and convenient to their minds. Thus, reality, like truth itself, is relative – each person sees his own reality and arrives at his own truth.

I was also intrigued – my sensibilities were pleased – by the sequence of words, 'Truth is no stranger'. I used those words as my Title and proceeded to 'build' the poem. My first two lines, I decided, must read,

'Truth is no stranger'
To falsehood and to fable.

The element of paradox is preserved and enhanced by the words 'falsehood' – which is directly opposed to truth – and by 'fable' or a made-up story, a fiction. The novelist often attempts to express 'truth' through a story, a fable. However, most readers regard fables as not-true stories. Fables are entertainments for children. If we look deeper, we discover that fables are 'carriers' of truth. Fables are a look deep into the heart.
My next two lines read:

The weak are no strangers
To the strong and the able.

My search for a rhyme to 'fable' takes me to 'able', that is, the strong. So our third line must be about 'the weak'. Stanzas, and indeed, whole poems are often written from the end backward to the beginning. We have completed the first stanza, and the mind plays around with other paradoxes. After a bit of experimentation on the draft page, I come up with:

Science is no stranger
To myth and mystery.

Science is 'knowledge' and the search for knowledge, or truth, or reality. Myth and mystery are their antitheses. The function of scientific investigation is to turn mystery (the unknown) into the known (truth). Einstein was forever intrigued by mystery, which he regarded as a thing of wonder. Note the alliteration in these two lines, the 's' sound in the first, the 'm' sound in the second.
We need 'history' as a rhyme for 'mystery', and, working backward again, we arrive at,

The future is no stranger
To the past of history.

The next two stanzas follow easily, and you see the mind at play: Ice is no stranger/To the heat of the fire.
We try 'the night' next.

The night is no stranger
To the dawn and the dew.

> The many are no stranger
> To the sparse and the few.

We conclude with the stanza on 'the sky'.

> The sky is no stranger
> To the bottom of the sea.
> The slave is no stranger
> To the master and the free.

Alliteration is rampant in the first three lines – the 's' sound again. And so the poem is concluded. We should not analyze too closely, lest we destroy the whole. However, I have gone into sufficient detail with this one poem, or set of stanzas, to show the mind of the creator at work. We have begun with a single phrase – 'truth is no stranger' – and have created a complete composition. Alliteration is as useful in prose as it is in poetry!

Finally, let me turn to the 'title' poem of this volume – 'Designs'. This is the 'key' poem, the one which comes closest to that magic we have heard about. I began with the final stanza; indeed, with the last two lines. The stanza reads:

> Each society designs
> Its cities and its states.
> Each man's eye designs the world
> Each man's mind creates.

The poem was suggested to me by a single line from the American poet, Howard Nemerov: 'The altering eye alters all.'

Each man's eye not only alters all, it actually *designs* the world 'Each man's mind creates.' We have brought together two fundamental truths. The world you live in is 'created' by your perception of it, by your interpretation of it in the light of your own individual experience. In short, It's all in your mind. What is reality? Your reality is quite different from my reality. Everything is relative to the 'creator' within your mind.

Turn now to the poem I call 'Designs'. Observe how, having begun with the end, I design the beginning and the middle. Enjoy the play of ideas and images. Perhaps what I have written in this introduction will assist you to understand and enjoy the other poems and verses you read in future.

PART I

PROLOGUE

A Book For All Seasons

Go, little book, and give to all
The pleasure of these verses.

Let those who read remember and recall
Each golden memory.

Let not it stay deserted in the hall,
Alone upon the shelf,

But open lie in the spring and in the fall,
A book to warm in winter.

Go, little book, and give to all
A summer of content.

**

(A double asterisk in the lower left corner of the page indicates that the poem above has a Note in a special section at the back of the book.)

A List Of What I Think I Am

Calm,
Cooperative,
Assertive and articulate,
And brave up to a point.

Cool,
Capable,
Inclined to kindliness,
And sinuous in every joint.

Carefree,
Conscientious,
Alert to opportunity,
Willing to accept but never to appoint.

Candid,
Creative,
Impervious to risk,
Willing to pray but never to anoint.

A Photograph

A photograph
Takes a moment prisoner
And puts it in a frame.

A photograph
Captures motion and
Imprints it on the brain.

A photograph
Takes magic and
Assigns to it a name.

A photograph
To color is
What a cloud is to rain.

A photograph
To light is
What link is to chain.

A photograph
Finds beauty in
A face forever plain.

A photograph
Is art when
Genius fans the flame.

The Artist

Every one a student is,
Never two the same.
Every one a viewer is,
Unique in eye and brain.

Every one accumulates,
Analyzes and compiles.
Every one a searcher is,
In ancient books and files.

Every one absorbent is,
Impressions flood the mind.
Every one a hunter is,
Each a style to find.

Every one a rebel is,
Defying discipline and form.
Every one an improviser is,
Uniqueness is the norm!

Bad Poets Plagiarize

If you want to be a poet —
This may come as a surprise,
Unless you already know it —
Bad poets plagiarize!

Like a farmer is a poet —
Sow the seed, then fertilize,
Cultivate as you grow it,
Till it measures up to size.

But the seeds the poet sows,
The ore the poet mines,
Go back, in poetry and prose,
To very ancient times.

There is, a wise man said,
Nothing new beneath the sun.
Every horse has been bred,
Every race has been run.

One principle applies —
This secret Time reveals —
Bad poets plagiarize,
But the good poet steals.

Of course, very good poets
Give credit where it's due.
But very good poets
Are very, very few!

The Brook Sings Its Melody

The brook sings its melody
  To the coming night,
The birds lift their colloquy
  To the dawning light.

The winds hum and sigh
  In the tops of trees,
The woods croon and cry
  In the evening breeze.

The waves waft their harmony
  To the listening shore,
The brook sings its melody
  As softly as before.

Come, Cicely, Let Us See

Come, Cicely, let us see
What leaf still hangs upon the tree,
What life has now in store for thee.

Time will not be ours forever,
Let's live before the sickle severs
The thread that holds us all together.

All sorrows tightly held are vain,
Hope leaps afresh like welcome rain,
Suns that set may rise again.

Take these verses in thy hand,
Take these pictures, firmly stand
Amid the trees, upon the land

Where soon the house you wish may rise,
Where summer sun and autumn skies
Will greet the sight before your eyes.

Envision here what you may find,
Imagine everything your mind
And heart desires. Do not decline

The gift I give, the love I bear.
Another year, and all that's fair
Will sprout upon this hill — I swear!

**

The Creative Mind

Saturation
Is the first
And fundamental law.

Feed in, feed in,
And fill the conscious mind
Until it expands and overflows.

Incubation
Is the second
And succeeding stage.

The great subconscious
Scans the field of data vast,
Mingles feeling with perception,

Winnows and
Eliminates the chaff,
Like a silent, swift computer.

Illumination
Leaps upward like
A flash of lightning fire.

Inspiration
Is the light that seems
From nothing to emerge.

Inspiration
Is the precious fruit
Of man's creative tree.

**

Designs

Each day's sun designs the shape
Of each light ray and shadow.
Each day's rain designs the cloak
Of each flower in the meadow.

Each night's dark designs
The heaven's starry host.
Each moon's tides design the face
Of each sea coast.

Each earthly birth designs
The fabric of a nation.
Each discovery designs
Each new creation.

Each society designs
Its cities and its states.
Each man's eye designs the world
Each man's mind creates.

**

Harvest

Promise is
  A rainbow in the sky.
Freedom is
  The right to defy.
Truth is
  Freedom's rally cry.
Courage is
  The willingness to try.
Love is
  A heart to signify.
Life is
  A cause to glorify.
Beauty is
  'The harvest of a quiet eye.'
A poem is
  To hold that harvest high.

**

I Am Hard To Satisfy

I am hard to satisfy,
But a melody will do it,
If the song has a lilt
And brightness running through it.

I am hard to satisfy,
But a sailing ship will do it,
If there's wine and port aboard
And a pretty maid to crew it.

I am hard to satisfy,
But a candy bar will do it,
If my jaws and my teeth
Are strong enough to chew it.

I am hard to satisfy,
But a picture show will do it,
If the picture is a mystery
With a plot to clue it.

I am hard to satisfy,
But a book of verse will do it,
If the critics don't complain
When they finally review it.

If The Color Means

If blue means fidelity,
Then I am blue for you.
If yellow means maturity,
Then I am yellow, too.

If green means productivity,
Then I'm as green as green can be.
If red means quick activity,
Then guilty is my plea.

If gray means a cloudy day,
Then I will pray for rain.
If brown means wheat or hay,
I'll harvest both again.

If purple means a mountain view,
Then I will climb the mountain high.
If orange means the sunshine, too,
Then I will worship sun and sky.

If You Tell Me Why

If you tell me why
The poem cannot be writ,
 I'll tell you why
 I think that I
 Can write if it I try.

If you tell me why
The song cannot be sung,
 I'll tell you why
 I think that I
 Can sing it if I try.

If you tell me why
The dream cannot come true,
 I'll tell you why
 I think that I
 Can make it if I try.

If you tell me why
The mountain can't be climbed,
 I'll tell you why
 I think that I
 Can climb it if I try.

In Praise Of Plagiarism

If you can't compose, assimilate or copy,
   Snatch a rose from Bartlett's garden.
If you can't purloin, be a warden,
   Each minted coin is gold on either side.
Choose the head, or take for yours the bride
   Someone else has shed. He owns the word
Who clasps it like a much beloved brother.
   It best is heard when stolen from another.

**

Mi Casa Es Su Casa

Mi casa es su casa,
  You know what I mean,
Mi casa es su casa,
  I keep it oh so clean.

Mi casa es su casa,
  Morning, noon and night,
Mi casa es su casa,
  You have every right.

Mi casa es su casa,
  The food is oh so good.
Mi casa es su casa,
  If come you only would.

Mi casa es su casa,
  My very last appeal,
Mi casa es su casa,
  Our kingdom, oh so real.

Mi casa es su casa,
  My house upon the hill,
Mi casa es su casa,
  If come you only will.

**

Morning, Noon and Eventide

At morn, with breaking dawn,
The darkness lies in tatters.

At noon the sun is high,
And light is all that matters.

At eventide, colors smear the sky,
As when a painter's palette shatters.

Reluctant Night

Reluctant night
Accepts the day's acquittal.
How pale the light,
The shadows noncommittal!

The moon rides above
The dark horizon.
How shy the stars
That roam the skies at random!

The birds flutter down
Amid the waiting leaves.
How sad the sound
As the darkness grieves!

Reluctant night!
The fragrant day is done.
How swift aroma's flight
When the race is run!

Reluctant night
Hides the face of sorrow.
How longs our dimming sight
For the coming of the morrow!

**

Some Say

Some say
That love is blind,
But I don't mind,
I'll love anyway!

Some say
That work's a grind,
But that is fine,
I'll work anyway!

Some say
You're what you eat,
Salty, sour or sweet —
But I'll eat anyway!

Some say
The law's not fair,
But I don't care,
I'll try anyway!

Some say
The race is fixed,
But the horse I've picked,
I'll bet anyway!

Some say
You cannot win,
But count me in,
I'll play anyway!

Somewhere

Somewhere there must be a road
   To the Nowhere Sea.
Somewhere there must be a land
   Outside geography.

Somewhere there must be a leaf
   On the Nonesuch tree.
Somewhere there must be a garden
   Outside reality.

**

Spending

I have been profligate of dreams,
   Spending midnight hours
   Seeking pleasure's bowers,
   Hunting fragile flowers,
   Enduring hardship's showers.
I have been profligate of dreams.

I have been profligate of hopes,
   Filling beauty's chest,
   Imagining the best,
   Passing every test,
   Working without rest.
I have been profligate of hopes.

I have been profligate of love,
   Dispensing my affection
   On every connection,
   Seeking satisfaction
   In senseless attraction.
I have been profligate of love.

I have been profligate of money,
   Borrowing and lending,
   Recklessly extending,
   All the while defending
   Injudicious spending.
I have been profligate of money.

'I have been profligate of happiness,'
   Drinking it like wine,
   Unable to confine
   The flow, or to assign
   Limits in space or in time.
'I have been profligate of happiness.'

**

Surprise

A poem should surprise,
Keats, the poet, said.
Every morning I arise,
To greet the day ahead.
Every morning a surprise,
Every day a newly-wed.

Scientists contend, Surprise
Is a universal ploy.
C. S. Lewis adds, 'Surprise
Is life's greatest joy!'
And the same applies
To every girl and boy.

The truth, no one denies,
Is the thing we must enhance.
The natural world relies
On randomness and chance.
Each discovery, a surprise!
Each connection, a romance!

**

Tell Me

Tell me
Where might a refuge be
From all of life's complexity.

Tell me
Where might a haven be
For minds in deep perplexity.

Tell me
Where might an Eden be
To satisfy society.

Tell me
Where might a churchyard be
For solitude and piety.

Things That Truly I Deplore

Astrology
And horoscopes
That fit a hundred million.
Pesky window envelopes
And budget deficits that top a billion.
Plants that always get the blight,
And curlers worn in a store.
Anchor persons wearing black or white,
And jokes I've heard twenty times before.

Cigarettes,
And alcohol
In all its different forms.
Ignorance of protocol,
And lightning bolts in summer storms.
Cats and dogs on public streets,
And lions that refuse to roar.
Parents bragging on children's feats,
And a plush carpet on the kitchen floor.

Two Little Girls

Two little girls
    In a meadow playing,
    One in pink,
    Blue the other.

Two little girls
    By the brook a-straying,
    One is sister
    To the other.

Two young girls
    With long tresses,
    One head's red,
    Blonde the other.

Two young girls
    In long dresses,
    One a print,
    Plaid the other.

Two young girls
    Off to college,
    One in art,
    Math the other.

Two young girls,
    Out to view the foliage,
    One in a Lexus,
    Infinity the other.

**

PART II

NATURE

A List of Things That Birds Do

Swoop,
Dart and hum,
Eat and excrete,
Swallow water from a pool,
Sing their song like a choir,
Sit in a row on lengths of wire,
And build their nests in the spring.

Warble,
Float on air,
Mark their territory,
Flit from tree to tree,
Hop all about on tiny feet,
Look for food in the street,
And gobble insects on the wing.

Hoot,
Sleep at night,
Greet the dawn
With songs of praise,
Take a long winter's trip,
Scavenge scraps from a ship,
And call for crackers from a swing.

As

As weak as a kitten,
As strong as an ox,
As soft as a mitten,
As sly as a fox.

As dull as dirt,
As sharp as a thistle,
As rough as a cob,
As slick as a whistle.

As big as a barn,
As small as a flea,
As hot as Hades,
As cold as the sea.

As flat as slate,
As round as a ball,
As low as a snake,
As high as a wall.

As white as snow,
As black as ink,
As slow as a snail,
As quick as a wink.

As hard as a rock,
As soft as fleece,
As jagged as a saw,
As smooth as grease.

As short as a stick,
As tall as a tree,
Asleep as a slug.
As busy as a bee.

As limp as a leaf,
As taut as tin,
As pretty as a picture,
As ugly as sin.

As heavy as lead,
As light as a shell,
As shallow as a grave,
As deep as a well.

As loose as a goose,
As tight as a drum.
As green as an olive,
As ripe as a plum.

At Sundown

At sundown,
The day surrenders to the night,
The earth inhales the fading light.

At sundown,
The trees turn their shadows in,
The hoot-owl's lonely cries begin.

At sundown,
The birds hunt a sleepy tree,
The stars set sail on a wine-dark sea.

At sundown,
The wind leans against the moon,
The dawn dreams of coming soon.

At sundown,
The clouds pull the covers up,
Darkness spills from Merlin's cup.

**

Color Is The Key

Color is the key that nature uses —
Delightful duty.
Each month a different color chooses —
Unlocking beauty!

January's white with snow again.
February, bright with ice's silver sheen.
March is violet with windy rain.
April coats the earth with green.

May is pink, the poet said.
June's fav'rite tone is blue.
July prefers a brilliant red.
August, brown — a burnished hue.

September chooses harvest yellow.
October turns the trees to gold.
November's rust — the fields lie fallow.
December's gray with winter cold.

Day

The light
Of dawn shut tight the door
And locked
The vault of night.
The stars
Went out, like dust swept off the floor.
The moon
Grew pale, as if in fright.

The day
Awoke — from its bed arose.
The sky
Drew on its cloak of blue.
The clouds
Assumed their morning pose.
The wind
Puffed out its cheeks and blew.

**

The Desert

That vast
Deserted territory
  Between the cactus and
  The clouds, the boundless floor
  Below the tableland.

The sun
Spills its fire upon
  The scrubby, rocky hills,
  Liquid heat that stuns
  And very often kills.

The ranches
Have no Devil's Rope
  For fences, and horses
  Have no halters. Cattle
Roam uncharted courses.

In summer,
Saguaros stand like signal men,
  Thick upon the land,
  Telegraphing heat
  Across the tawny sand.

The Devil
Stirs the dust in sudden
  Upward, twisting flights,
  Before it settles down,
  Declaring squatter's rights.

Beauty,
Held for ransom by
  The fiery summer heat,
  Wins its freedom at
  The mountain's shady feet.

The night,
A predator that steals
   The day's reluctant light,
   Protects the creatures that
   Regard the day with fright.

The petroglyphs
Are more than pictures on
   The walls of pink sandstone.
   Not mere symbols they —
   They stand for life alone.

A lizard,
Camouflaged by stripes,
   Lies flat upon the blade —
   The Spanish bayonet
   Provides its wanted shade.

Lightning
Forks the autumn sky.
   Nature's brittle steel
   Strikes the desert's flint,
   Makes the landscape reel.

Autumn winds
Sweep the mesa bare,
   Chase the tumbleweed,
   Stir the whirling dust,
   Scatter desert seed.

The frost
At morning gives the cold
   A brilliant diamond edge,
   Sews a coat of silver
   About the mountain ledge.

At night,
When winter cold descends,
   The yucca and mesquite

Quake and shiver in
Defense against defeat.

Winter storms
Slash the desert sky,
　Winds and waterfalls
　Carve the figures deep
　In layered canyon walls.

Winter's cold
Strikes the locust and
　The willow wattle trees.
　Winter winds bring down
　Their crisp and yellow leaves.

The dawn
Washes up upon the shores
　Of every desert morning.
　The light of spring reveals
　The desert new a-borning.

The sun
Announces early spring,
　The vernal equinox —
　And sudden multitudes
　Of pink and purple phlox.

In the
Lexicon of spring,
　The most descriptive word
　Is serendipity —
　Flower, plant and bird.

The rains
Of spring in cadence fall,
　The sun in splendor shines,
　And hosts of yellow flowers
　Adorn the cacti's spines.

The clouds
That nightly gather,
    Like mists in nature's jars,
    Obscure the blinking planets,
    Ride herd upon the stars.

The desert
Wears its tawny tan
    All the year around,
    Except those fleeting weeks
    When colors so abound.

The pods,
Suspended on the limbs
    Of acacia and mesquite,
    Scent the desert air
    With aromas sweet.

The warm
Winds blow softly through
    The slender elder trees,
    Whose silent seeds spin down,
    As nature's law decrees.

**

Fearful Nature

The wind moans,
The trees tremble,
The coward moon
Hides behind a cloud.

The waves roar,
The earth shakes,
The stars flee
Before the cosmic wind.

The waters fall,
The rocky rapids foam,
The shadows grovel
On the valley floor.

The air thickens,
The skies darken,
The tropic seas spawn
A torrid storm.

The fleeting stars pierce the dark,
Lightning 'scribes an awesome arc.

Fearful nature speaks its mind aloud,
The coward moon slips behind a cloud.

Gravity

Gravity is the master force
That drives the universe and holds
The stars in their course,
The planets 'tween their poles.

    Gravity, in Newton's view,
    Is the force that draws
    Object-one to object-two,
    One of nature's laws.

Galileo did his best
To convince one and all,
That objects large, in his test,
Fall as slow as objects small.

    Gravity's the most perverse,
    And the very weakest force
    In the universe,
    According to my source.

Einstein has it bending space,
Slowing down the speed of time,
Says that it will win the race
With light by the width of a dime.

    A Black Hole, Hawking relates,
    Is that place where gravity
    Is so strong that no light escapes —
    Such is G's intensity!

**

It Is Time

It is time to walk the woods
   And look at leaves.
It is time to harvest hay
   And stack the sheaves.

It is time the suckling calves
   Drink their fill.
It is time the winter winds
   Waft their chill.

It is time to feed the fire
   With lengths of logs.
It is time to exorcise
   The mental fogs.

It is time to see the light
   Slip in streams.
It is time to set your ship
   Adrift in dreams.

**

Like

A bird
Is like a leaf
On a copper tree.

A wagon wheel
Is like the moon at full
In a wooden sky.

A cloud
Is like a lamb
On a field of blue.

A ship
Is like a spoon
On a silver sea.

Like The First

Sunlight is streaming,
Moonlight is beaming,
  Like the first sunlight,
  Like the first moonbeams.

Songbirds are singing,
Church bells are ringing,
  Like the first songbirds,
  Like the first church bells.

Spring winds are blowing,
Sea currents flowing,
  Like the first spring winds,
  Like the first sea currents.

Raindrops are falling,
Morning larks calling,
  Like the first raindrops,
  Like the first morning larks.

**

The Months Of Spring

March!
Be thou ever blessed with rains that fall
Upon the fallow ground,
And winds that scatter all
The seeds of spring around.

April!
Be thou ever blessed with bees that carry
Pollen on their feet,
With birds that sing their morning
Madrigals so sweet.

May!
Be thou ever graced with beauty from
The faces of the flowers
That crowd the meadows green
And stock the sunny bowers.

The Moon

The moon,
Like a mirror, swallows light,
Shapes the shadows of the night.

The moon,
Like an eagle, rides the wind,
Teaches trees how to bend.

The moon,
Like a warrior, holds as pawn
The light in search of dawn.

The moon,
Like the sun and the rain,
Bleaches wheat on the plain.

The moon,
Like a weaver on a stool,
Unravels darkness from a spool.

The moon,
Like an actor in a run,
Takes its cue from the sun.

The moon,
Like a swan upon the lake,
Leaves a shadow in its wake.

The moon,
Like a sailor on the strand,
Leaves its footprints in the sand.

Nature

Sun and rain
Tend the naked earth.
Spring and summer
Witness every birth.

Nature never does
Bestow a pedigree.
Every creature,
High and low, is aristocracy.

Nature strives
For perfect form,
But soon gives up the fight —
Approximation is the norm.

Nature's plans,
As chaotic as the sea,
But Nature's song
Has a harmony.

Reality appears to be
A sea of random shimmers,
But in the deeper depths
Order dimly glimmers.

**

Nature's Irregularities

We are told
That architect of English landscapes,
Capability Brown,
Much preferred
Nature's incalculable irregularities
To formal gardens.

It may well be
That architect of all nature,
That great and
Universal artist,
Composed a super symmetry, as yet
Unknown to man.

The visible world
Is not matter, the story goes,
Nor is it spirit.
The visible world
Is simply — or complexly — the invisible
Organization of energy.

Partial symmetries
Are all that Yang and Lee can show;
Weinberg no more.
Not even Glashow
Or Gell-Mann have mounted to the top
Rung on the ladder

Of present theories.
New tools are daily added to the inventory
Of men's machines:
Computers compound
Knowledge, and super telescopes will
Expedite discovery.

They may together,
On some near or far tomorrow, reveal the structure
And the history
Of this strange
And eerie cosmos which so rapidly
Continues to expand.

There seem to be
Endless fluctuations of energy and matter,
A frightening chaos
In both the fields
Of space and time, random eddies of
Ghostly particles

That may not exist.
Far below nature's majestic order
Lies a random base,
A godly grammar
That governs mutation and sets the
Course of evolution.

**

Nature's Law

The day is fairest when it's new,
Jewels rarest when they're few.
Not one flaw
In nature's law.

Light is clearest in the morn,
Love is dearest when it's born.
Look with awe
On nature's law.

Nature never does deceive,
As long as ever you believe.
What you saw
Was nature's law.

Nature's will is nature's way,
Man will never nature sway.
Strong of jaw
Is nature's law.

All that which in nature flowers
Holds the switch to nature's powers.
Tooth-and-claw
Is nature's law.

Artist's arrows go askew,
Nature's arrows never do.
It's the law,
Nature's law.

**

Never As

One green field is never as
　Green as another.

One river gorge is never as
　Gorgeous as another.

One high peak is never as
　High as another.

One silver cloud is never as
　Silver as another.

One famous man is never as
　Famous as another.

One fickle friend is never as
　Fickle as another.

One happy mother is never as
　Happy as another.

One pretty girl is never as
　Pretty as another.

One clever poet is never as
　Clever as another.

Perhaps

Perhaps the azure sky
　Taught the bluebirds blue.

Perhaps — one can't deny —
　It taught the bluebell too.

Perhaps the setting sun
　Taught the redbird red.
Perhaps the colors run
　When the sky is bled.

Perhaps the falling snow
　Taught the white egret.
Perhaps the water's flow
　Is the whitest yet.

Perhaps the autumn leaves
　Taught the owl his brown.
Perhaps the duck believes
　They colored all his down.

Rain

The rain descends in drops,
Or comes in thundershowers,
The cloud's effluvium
Nourishes the crops,
Encourages the flowers
To blossom in the sun.

Clouds carry rain,
Which they accumulate
From the sea's evaporation.
The rain descends on the plain,
On every town in every state,
And upon every nation.

But nature has a random way,
An arbitrary plan,
For the rain's distribution.
It falls on hardened clay,
On the loam of the fields, on the sand —
Each receives its contribution.

The waters tend to flow
Down to rivers and to lakes,
Tumbling swift, moving slow,
As invariably it makes
Its way to the seas.

Russian Evening

The day winds down
With a quiet swish of evening stillness.

The wind rattles the garden —
The brittle litter of dead flowers.

Sparrows sit, like dark berries,
On black branches.

The rising moon hugs the sky,
The waters of the lake doze.

The hoot of the owl 'comes bold,
The dust in the yard grows cold.

**

The Seasons

Summer's still supreme in
  Every single southern state
  Along the magic border
From Florida to California.

Autumn's still the season mild,
  Residing most enchantingly
  In all the mountain states
From Vermont to Tennessee.

Winter holds its hostages — every
  Point above the Mason-Dixon line,
  Gripping all the northern states
From Michigan to frigid Oregon.

Spring delights in travelling
  Along a route, Mexico to Canada,
  Stopping momentarily at every state
From Mississippi to New York.

Shade Trees

When we see a grassy yard
  Adorned with swaying shade trees,
We know, with sudden pleasure, why
  God simply up and made trees.

When we see a city street
  Enhanced with rows of shade trees,
We really can't imagine why
  There are those who upbraid trees.

When we see a river bank
  Trimmed with lovely tall trees,
We know in spring and summer that
  We'll soon enjoy the fall trees.

When we see the mountain slopes,
  Almost too steep to grow trees,
We know that in the winter time
  They'll wear a coat of snow trees.

Shadows

Shadows,
Sleeping silently,
  Rise from the earth,
  Become mature
  Minutes after birth.

Shadows,
Long, thin fingers
  In night's tangled hair,
  Emerge boldly from
  The dark, adjacent lair.

Shadows
Hovering on the edge,
  Await the pending dawn,
  Sending scouts ahead
  Before the night is gone.

Shadows
Send a shiver up
  The mountain's rocky spine,
  Ride the valley's nerves
  And vex the hills's incline.

Shadows
Creep along the wall,
  In search of any gate
  Of entry to
  A scenic gardenscape.

The Silent Seasons

The budding spring
Crept in with a sudden softness.

The silver sun
Spread 'cross the floor of summer.

The autumn wind
Scattered seeds at random.

The winter snow
Fell silent as a dream.

**

The Sun

That great ball of fire, the sun,
Consists of giant masses
Of incandescent gasses
That boil and spew and run

Along its surface like loops
Of burning rope, convecting
Like a hot oven, affecting
Every planet, singly and in groups.

Sunspots and shooting flares
Of electrons and protons
Create solar winds, X-Rays and photons,
Magnetic fields in pairs.

The sun, our closest star,
Is itself a laboratory
Which every observatory
Studies from afar

To learn about the universe,
Of which the earth is part.
The sun's the horse that pulls the cart,
Shedding rays for better or for worse.

The sun bestows light and heat,
Sustains mankind and everything
That lives, every bird on the wing,
Every plant and fruit we eat.

The solar winds shape
Earth's magnetic fields,
And the sun's power yields
The energies that create

This world where we strive
To hold a steady course,
To harness every force
We need to stay alive.

The sun's power rays
Drive this planet's weather,
Very like a very clever
Computer full of wily ways.

Sun, Moons And Stars

The morning sun
Revels in promiscuity,
Shedding rays
Wherever they will fall.

    The crescent moon,
    Sharpened by acuity,
    Casting shadows
    On whatever wall.

The evening stars,
Across the void's vacuity,
Blink their coded signals,
Heaven's crystal ball.

Sun, Moon And Stars — 2

The sun,
With no intent to barter,
Spent
Lavishly from its cosmic store.

The moon
Lent power to the water,
Holding
No collateral from the willing shore.

The stars,
With neither lease nor charter,
Agreed
To shine forever and forevermore.

Sun, Moon And Stars — 3

The sun, when it sets,
  Is a picture of perfection.
The moon oft abets
  Its silvery reflection.

The stars, newly born,
  Are shining points of light.
The dark before the dawn
  Is hostage to the night.

The sun greens the grass
  With its silent rays,
The moon prefers to pass
  The house in which it stays.

The stars blink in code
  Their messages to earth,
Revealing their abode
  And the time of their birth.

Thunder and Lightning

Ancient man discovered fire,
 Far back in olden days,
When nature's vivid wire
 Set a tree or two ablaze.

Fire was evil — once the view,
 Terrifying beast and man.
But fires purify and renew –
 Nature's secret plan.

Thunder's nature's noisy clerk,
 But truth to tell,
Lightning does the work,
 Lightning rings the bell.

Thunder tears the fabric of the sky,
 But lightning brings the rain.
Thunder causes birds to fly,
 Lightning never works in vain.

Thunder claps the mountain sides,
 Lightning sets the clouds aglow.
The coming storm on thunder rides,
 Lightning steals the weather show.

'Where shall we three meet again,'
 The witches shrieked in William's play,
'In thunder, lightning or in rain?'
 Where do witches meet today?

**

Trees

In spring the dogwood blossoms
Sparkle in the verdant forests
Of Olympic Peninsula,
And hemlocks rise in a glory of green.

    In summer the chestnut trees
    Display their coats of gold.
    Hawaii smells the fragrant blossoms
    Of the rainbow shower trees.

In autumn the aspens and the scarlet oaks
Signal the coming of the sylvan harvest.
The desert cottonwoods dazzle,
And the golden sugar maples glow.

    In winter the sun-lit snow
    Crowns the lordly elms,
    And in the west the redwoods
    Touch the cold December sky.

The Vagaries Of Nature

The sun at time of setting
   Is more beautiful than most:
Colors rampant on a field
To which the sky is host.

Breezes howsoever light,
   And winds, howsoever spent,
Will invariably unplumb
   The rain's straight descent.

Shining on a foreign coast,
   The moon casts its shadows,
Like a many-fingered ghost,
   In strange and subtle patterns.

The vagaries of nature
   Are in paintings most pronounced,
Watch the ways that rays of light
Wrap an object round about!

**

When

When the universe
In one electric moment
Declares itself —

When the lightning
Prowls at night
Along the canyon rim —

When the sun
Cuts corridors through the clouds,
Dark as loam —

When descending waters
Fall from coal-black cliffs
Into silver basins —

When the setting sun
Makes a mirror
Of the lake —

When shooting stars
Streak the silent sky
In the dead of night —

When the winter snow
Coats the limber boughs
Of the forest pine —

When pods of leaping dolphins
Glowing pearly pink,
Arc across the waters —

When The Trees Put On Their Joseph Coats

By the middle of October,
When the harvest's mostly over,
The trees put on their fall attire,
Full as bright as forest fire.

The birches swiftly change to gold,
Anticipating winter's cold.
The scarlet maples, red as cherries,
The dogwoods' crimson berries.

The sweetgums wear a vivid gown,
The oaks assume a tawny brown.
The aspens and the willows share
The yellow which the elms and ginkoes wear.

The leaves no longer drink the sun,
And the colors tend to run.
The basswoods shift from green to bronze,
Dropping leaves on silver ponds.

**

Wide As A Dream

The night is a black and restless sea,
Dark as doom.
The sky is a continent of clouds,
Gray as a shawl.
Space is a sea of solitude,
Light as a loom.
Time is an endless continuum,
Round as a ball.

    The earth is a blanket of cotton and silk,
    Frail as burrs.
    The wind is a seamless sheet,
    Clear as a bell.
    The moon is a silver sailing ship,
    Shiny as spurs.
    The universe is a cosmic swimming hole,
    Deep as a well.

Nature and art are a great collage,
Wide as a dream.
The stars are a colored mantle of light,
Brights as eyes.
The poles are curtains of snow and ice,
Cold as fate.
Science is a lab with an open end,
Lethal as lies.

**

Wind And Water

Wind and
Water interlocked —
  As close as siblings are,
  Clearly nature's cousins —
  As planet is to star.

Water rose
As mist above the sea.
  Falling back to earth,
  It joined the sun
  And gave the rainbow birth.

The wind
Gathered all its force,
  Hurled the desert sand
  Across the desert rocks,
  Formed the mesa land.

The water
Rose in crater lakes,
  Dropped in mighty falls,
  Took a million years
  To cut through canyon walls.

Wind and
Water ever wrestle
  One against the other,
  Striving to become
  Nature's elder brother.

The Wind

The wind at dawn
Blows the mist
Hither and yon, hither and yon.

The wind at noon
Stirs the heat
Late and soon, late and soon.

The wind at night
Shifts the shadows
Left and right, left and right.

The wind in spring
Inspires the birds
To wake and sing, to wake and sing.

The wind in summer
Warms the air
Here and there, here and there.

The wind in fall
Sways the trees
Short and tall, short and tall.

The wind in winter
Blows the snow
To and fro, to and fro.

The Wind — 2

The wind
Comes off Pacific waters,
Wafts the waves
To the waiting shore.

The wind
Roars through mountain passes,
Croons across rocky ravines,
On its journey to the plains.

The wind
Is a messenger
That sings of coming storms,
Whistling away its fears.

The wind
Stirs the desert sands,
Swirls the tumbleweed,
Sculpts the limestone hills.

The wind
Swishes through the grasses,
Rustles the trembling leaves
Of cherry and cottonwood trees.

The wind
Swirls the mountain mists
Above the broadleaf forests
Of smoky Applachia.

The wind
Sweeps the city streets
Within the granite canyons,
Moans across Manhattan.

The Winds Of Spring

The light of dawn is faintly glowing,
  The tractor motor's going,
  Keeps the harrow-towing,
  The sun its warmth bestowing,
O, the winds of Spring are blowing!

At morn the jaunty rooster's crowing,
  The flowers' faces showing,
  The cows at night are lowing,
  The glowworms brightly glowing,
O, the winds of Spring are blowing!

The meadow grass so quickly growing,
  The hay may soon need mowing.
  The cotton calls for hoeing,
  The creek is freely flowing,
O, the winds of Spring are blowing!

**

PART III

TRAVEL

A List Of Places I Have Never Been
But Maybe You Have

The isle of Bali,
And the city of Baku,
India's New Delhi,
And Lima in Peru.

Beautiful Lahore,
The Horn and Patagonia,
Clean Singapore,
And New Caladonia.

The Cape of Good Hope,
The steppes of Siberia,
The office of the Pope,
And the tip of Algeria.

The beach at Acapulco,
The city of Kompong,
The deserts of Morocco,
And the races in Hongkong.

The home of George the Fourth,
And the Bay of Fundy,
The Pole called The North,
And Moscow on a Monday.

Carlsbad Caverns

Across the arid west,
Beneath a boundless sky,
Runs a hot strip of road
To the gently rising ridges

Of the Guadalupe Mountains,
And on the eastern flank
Nature has performed a miracle —
The Caverns of Carlsbad.

Limestone rock grips the caverns
In its giant embrace.
Far below a soaring cathedral lies
Entombed, its antechambers

Scattered round the perimeter.
And the acid waters drip,
As they have slowly dripped
For a hundred million years.

Great stone stalactites cling
To the cavern's ceiling,
While stalagmites rise from
The floor, like melting candles.

Eight hundred feet below,
The Big Room lies,
A single fourteen-acre cavern,
A chamber filled with muffled voices.

Colored lights transform
The underground wonderland.
Stalactites join together
In the Queen's Chamber,
Like billowing golden draperies.

At night, from the cavern's maw
Comes a cloud of black wings
And a dozen million bats
Scavenge the insect-polluted air.

China Is Dark

The world will long remember
The blood-streaked student faces,
The prostrate bodies crushed,
The bath of violence in Tiananmen Square
On the third and fourth of June.

    The convoy trucks ablaze,
    The tanks afire at night,
    The river of blood in Tiananmen Square.
    One bleeding student said,
    'China is dark, China is dead!'

The world will long remember
The lone, anonymous man,
The white-shirted man
Who stood before a lumbering column
Of silent, steel tanks,

    In defiance shouted, 'Why are you here?
    My city is in chaos!'
    But the People's Army
    Sprayed the square with bullets and blood,
    And the river became a flood.

The world will long remember
Those days in Tiananmen Square,
The wrath of Deng, the shadow of Stalin,
The power of the gun
Against the will of the people.

    Bloodbaths breed revulsion,
    China is dark,
    Communism is dying,
    The Old Men know,
    As the winds of democracy blow.
**

The City At Night

What a bright coat of light
The city wears at night!

The brilliant glow, as of noon,
Hides the slow-rising moon.

Towers rise like mighty spars,
Each a-tip with winking stars.

Vans and cars and busses share
The thoroughfare.

Avenues, parks and city lots
Are blankets of yellow dots.

The narrow runways lie —
Lighted pathways in the sky.

Spread below, mile on mile,
The lighted city's lovely smile!

**

El Niño

When, in South Pacific Islands,
   Where men in battles fought,
And gentle waves lap the sands,
   Atmospheric pressure drops to naught.

The hot tropic sun
   Heats the surface waters,
And warming Trade Winds run
   From west to eastern quarters,

From Easter Island's cliffs
   To the shores of Peru,
And the colored waters shift
   From green to vivid blue.

But every seven years or so,
   The pressure zones reverse:
The high at Darwin turns to low,
   And then is born the curse,

The wind they call *EL NIÑO*,
   The wind that devils host,
The dreaded wind that flows
   To California's northern coast.

EL NIÑO, like the jet stream,
   Takes control where e'er it goes,
Determines, it would seem,
   The path the weather flows.

English Journey

At last take leave of London,
   City on a river.
Become a happy wanderer
   From Waterloo and Wembley.
Remember rue in Regent's Park,
   The bells of St. Clement's,
Tower Bridge, Trafalgar Square.
   Take the country air, cool as rain.

Heed the gates of stately houses,
   Linger long at Walden Bury —
Sheets of water stitched with light,
   Swans a-gliding by the shore.
Statues dot the broad green garden,
   Beds of flowers, vats of colour —
Daffodils and rhododendron
   Bloom along the border.

Low white stiles cross grey fences,
   Winds sweep seas of tawney barley.
Royston Road leads to Newmarket,
   Horses gallop on the Downs,
Heads held high, velvet nostrils all aquiver.
   Chestnut trees hide the trails
Leading back to scattered barns.
   Restless currents frighten birds.

Blowing clouds scud the sky,
   Willows weep along the Cam.
Churches grow on tombstoned greens,
   Arches finely etched in Norman towers,
Gleaming windows cut from amber rock.
   The nave is dark and cool,
Music whispers from the organ loft.
   The day is blessed with sudden sun.

Gentle limestone slopes climb
   The Cotswold hills.
Sheep glean the shining meadows,
   Lambs leap in awkward gambol.
Silver streams, ducks a-waddling,
   Tiny bridges built of stone,
Neat-thatched houses on a reedy river.
   Trees with feather tops.

Lymm lies along the way,
   Wigon and Walton, on the road to Windermere.
Far off ridges speak of rivers,
   A mill, a cottage with dovecote,
A timbered courtyard, an inn on a rocky terrace.
   A stop for tea and mint cake.
Rain falls gently on the sentient soil,
   Perfumes of England float softly on the air.

Ambleside tipped the lake,
   Bowness was closer by the mere.
Rows of rocky spines melt
   To blue and grey. Lacy waterfalls
Glisten on the flanks of cadenced fells.
   Sun glints on sudden spurts of stone.
Coppery beeches weave a wild tweed
   On the lake's leafy landscape.

Carlisle and Dumfries form the gates
   To Scotland's deepening dales.
Across the hanging valleys —
   Rocky hills smeared with lichen,
Rusty orange and brilliant green.
   Burnished sea of bracken,
Dark emerald, with hints of gold,
   Hummocks of heather on purple hillsides.

The day is opalescent with twilight,
The Castle gleams upon the hill.
The Firth reflects the dying rays.
Peace returns to Princes Street,
Darkness walks the Royal Mile.
Shadows rise from cooling stones
And shroud the Heart of Midlothian.
Night descends, quiet as ashes falling.

**

Glacier National Park

Jagged mountains tower
Above the forest wilderness,
Ice fields skyward curve,
Colors sharp, muted shade.

Lakes line the canyon depths,
Nestle in the arms of lofty valleys.
Forests climb high above the shore,
Meadows cling to mountain slopes.

Snowfields drape every ledge
And pocket. Glaciers slowly edge
Their downward way,
Compressing crusty earth.

Glaciers pluck boulders from
The ground and slowly grind
Through narrow valleys.
Matterhorns are born.

The gray-backed grizzly bears
Fish in frigid waters.
The antelope, like mountain goats,
Skip up the sheer cliff's face.

In summer, frothing waters flow
From the glacier's edge,
Cascading into cobbled creek beds,
Tumbling into lakes deep and cold.

Grand Canyon

Autumn comes early
To the lofty North Rim.
Quaking aspens in yellow flames.
The mile-deep chasm glows.

White winter snows mantle
Russet canyon walls.
Golden sun illuminates
Stark canyon shapes.

Brilliant colors spring to life
In wide canyon meadows
Near the green forest's edge.
Deer Creek carves the brown sandstone.

In the misty brightness
Before the coming storm,
The canyon's face is moody,
The sky foreboding, a rainbow arcs.

Follow winding Kaibab Trail,
Along suspension bridge,
Across the roaring Colorado,
To distant Phantom Ranch.

Ride sure-footed mules
Past the walls of cream and dusty rose,
From the rim to Roaring Springs.
Run the rapids in a rubber boat.

Crowds of gray-green trees
Billow downward to the desert floor,
Half as old as earth itself.
Vermilion limestone walls, winding river.

Iowa

Sun, like silver,
Coats the clouds after storm.
Barns, like churches,
Watch over aisles of corn.

Trees, like widows,
Weep along the river red.
Fields, like blankets,
Cover summer's bed.

Cows, like statues,
In utter silence stand.
Roads, like ribbons,
Bind the fruitful land.

Lakes, like mirrors,
Reflect the blue above.
Birds, like autumn leaves,
Scatter notes of love.

Journeys

Of all of man's activities,
   Journeys are perhaps the best,
   Journeys east, journeys west,
According to proclivities.

Many are the rewards
   Of frequent travelling,
   Such as the unravelling
Of nerves as sharp as swords.

Plan your journeys in detail
   But if you have TRIPLE-A,
   Let *them* tell you where to stay,
When to fly, when to sail.

Loudly calls the open road,
   Every map affords a clue,
   Highways red, highways blue,
Miles and mountains have a code.

You should never contemplate
   A journey without spouse or friend,
   Whose abilities extend
Beyond the urge to navigate.

I have travelled everywhere,
   Have the aches and pains to show,
   But there's another way to go,
Without the trouble or the fare.

Get a handy travel guide,
   Get an atlas or a map,
   Plotting journeys is a snap,
All the data is supplied.

On The Way To Santa Fe

Boundless sky,
Roadside crosses,
North on I-Two-Five,
Prickly plants abound,
On the way to Santa Fe.

North to the mountains,
Across the desert floor,
Canyon winds across the draw,
A town called San Antonio,
On the way to Santa Fe.

Ski slopes,
Adobe walls,
Pueblos on the hills,
A Reservation called Apache,
On the way to Santa Fe.

Piñon trees,
Quarter horses,
Snow geese flying,
A mountain called Sandia,
On the way to Santa Fe.

**

Petrified Forest

For two hundred million years
That great sculptor, Time,
With clay and water, created
A rainbow of earth, the Painted Desert.

Under deep seas, jungle trees
Lay for eons. With subsiding waters,
Sand and minerals deposited
Stone statues, the Petrified Forest.

Arizona grasslands
Suddenly part to reveal
A kaleidoscope of colors,
Trees turned to jewelled stone.

Across the broad Blue Mesa
The giant logs lie, like
Fallen pillars, souvenirs
Of the dim geologic past.

Tons of stone-crystal wood
Lie rooted in the rocky matrix,
Like unfinished sculptures.
Man and nature erode the petrified forest.

In the short silent spring,
Wildflowers coat the desert floor.
Yuccas bloom and gray cacti
Mingle with the desert grasses.

Redwoods

The Avenue of Giants
Winds along the River Eel,
Thirty miles of glory,
Coastal redwoods, old Sequoias.

Redwood giants connect earth
And sky. Rhododendrons cluster
Round the massive trunks.
Tan oaks and madrona live in shade.

The forest floor gleams
With blue blossom and wood rose,
With ferns of jungle green,
A tapestry of color.

Stately groves of redwood trees,
Richly wooded hills
On Feather River Canyon.
Quiet pools, roaring rapids.

The summer mists roll in
On ocean winds and currents.
Redwoods favor belts of fog
Along a rocky coast.

Yosemite

Ice is the master sculptor
Of grand Yosemite.
Half Dome is the monolith
High above the valley floor.

When winter snows melt in spring,
The Falls of Yosemite
Tumble into misty pools,
Waters shake the very ground.

Autumn wears her brightest clothes
In the Valley of Yosemite.
Conifers shed their somber mood,
Join the yellow aspens.

A mighty block of solid granite,
The largest in the world,
Stands like a sentinel.
Climbers scale El Capitan.

Hike a mile along Mist Trail
Up the verdant valley,
Vernal Falls is the jewel
In the crown of Yosemite.

Dark and fertile clouds hover
Over grand Yosemite.
Winter storms descend.
Bridleveil and Ribbon Falls.

PART IV

MORALS AND METAPHYSICS

The ABC's

'A' is for Answers,
   Which are what
   Everyone is looking for.
Answers to problems mathematical,
Answers to questions and queries,
Answers to matters statistical,
And when to eat mushrooms and berries.

'B' is for Basics,
   Which are what
   Everyone should get back to.
Basics from childhood,
Basics from school,
Basics from forest and wildwood,
And the golden rule.

'C' is for Creature,
   Which is what
   Everyone is, a creature
Searching for certitude,
Coping with chance,
Failing in fortitude,
Afraid of romance.

A Haunting Dream That Lingered

A haunting dream that lingered
  On the morning light.
A harvest moon that lingered
  Far beyond the night.

  A song that sweetly lingered
    On a wave of sound.
  An arrowhead that lingered
    On a desert mound.

A lofty love that lingered
  On the path of lust.
An autumn wind that lingered
  On a tongue of dust.

  A narrow road that lingered
    'Round a sloping bend.
  A lonely leaf that lingered
    On a winter wind.

The silent crowd that lingered
  At the tragic scene.
The driven ball that lingered
  On the level green.

  An early worm that lingered
    On the robin's beak.
  A setting sun that lingered
    On the mountain peak.

**

All

Often times
All is smooth,
But often
All is rough.

Often times
All sufficient is,
But often
All is not enough.

Often times
All is more,
But often
All is simply less.

Often times
All most serious is,
But often
All is jest.

**

A List Of Things Hard To Believe

Confidences,
Winning bets,
Walnut meat emerging whole,
And inexpensive motion-picture shows.

Aphrodisiacs,
Beginner's luck,
Commercials on TV,
And photographs of UFOs.

Testimony,
Wrestling matches,
Corporate balance sheets,
And the Market up at the close.

Lawyers,
First opinions,
Congressional committees,
And leading ladies who refuse to pose.

A List Of Things That Slip Away

Time,
Promises,
Money in the bank,
And shadows on the floor.

Lovers,
Resolutions,
Youth and middle-age,
And memories galore.

Mercury,
Moonlight,
Beads without a string,
And quotations by the score.

Jokes,
Jade earrings,
Honey in the comb,
And sounds you've heard before.

A Man Is More

A man is more
Than a muscle with a brain.
A man is more
Than a link in a chain.

A man is more
Than a record high balloon.
A man is more
Than a walk on the moon.

A man is more
Than his skills and his arts.
A man is more
Than the sum of his parts.

Apathy

Apathy is not a word
You'll find in Bartlett, John,
Which may result partly from
The meaning not inferred.

It's true that you may not
Have a passion for
That which cannot restore
Something long forgot.

Apathy's a total lack
Of animal or human feeling.
Apathy's a total sealing
Of the heart, a turning back

Of ardor and of love,
Never giving them a chance
To circumvent circumstance,
Impossible to move.

If there is one you must subdue,
A thing you wish to kill,
Then you simply fill
Your heart with apathy and rue.

Appearances

A thing is never what it seems,
Never what it claims to be,
And never will confess.
Everything a double has,
Assumes another shape,
Or wears another dress.

The flaming log, encased in fire,
Is really solar energy
From a cosmic store.
The diamond dazzles with its light,
Derived from tensive pressure on
Its deep and inner core.

Water plays a double game,
Ever different, yet the same,
Changes steam to ice.
But people are the centerpiece:
The human heart so evil is,
Yet often is so nice!

Artifice

Art
Inspired by artifice
Does not deserve the name.

Art
Inspired by nature
May justify the claim.

Beauty
Made by artifice
Is dross after fire.

Beauty
Made by nature
Is beauty to admire.

Culture
Built on artifice
Is shaky and unsure.

Culture
Built on history
May very well endure.

Drama
Built on artifice
Soon will fall apart.

Drama
Built on character
Reveals the human heart.

A Single

All life's light,
From a single sun.
All life's many,
From a single one.

All life's fire,
From a single spark.
All life's arrows
To a single mark.

All life's sweets,
From a single spring.
All life's beads
On a single string.

All life's hope,
From a single Son.
All life's many,
From a single one.

Aspects Of Childhood

In spring the buds are closely curled,
As in childhood's secret world.

The summer sun's early rise
Lights the fire in childhood's eyes.

Waters fall in rainbow spray,
As in childhood's autumn play.

Winter snow feeds the brook
That sings the songs in childhood's book.

Childhood's time has no end,
For time itself is childhood's friend.

Childhood's magic is simplicity —
Innocence enfolded in mystery.

Childhood's skies are forever blue.
Childhood's dreams forever true.

Awkward

Awkward
Is the child of early age,
  Who attempts to rise
  From his knees to his feet,
  And succeeds, with great surprise.

Awkward
Is the boy who approaches
  Puberty, the girl as she
  Looks to the moment when
  They first encounter — she and he.

Awkward
Is a girl with a glove
  And a baseball in her hand.
  Awkward is as awkward does,
  Why can't she throw like a man?

Auk-ward
Is perhaps, per chance,
  Possibly the ward — I think —
  Of that peculiar, flightless bird,
The auk, unless the auk's extinct.

Awkwardness
Is a brother to embarrassment,
  One the other follows close,
  Two sides of a single coin,
  Two medicines in a dose.

If awkward
You still are, never fret.
  This is as close to awkwardness
  As you possibly can get!

**

Beauty

Beauty is the feather on the wings
    That lift one above.
Beauty is the harp that sings
    The song of earthly love.

Beauty is the fire that burns
    Like sunlight on the sea.
Beauty is desire that turns
    An hour into eternity.

Beauty is the light behind the shadow
    That falls upon the ground.
Beauty is the sweet and mellow
    Melody that hovers all around.

Beauty is the scent upon the breeze
    When spring begins to glow.
Beauty is the dance of autumn leaves
    Before the winter snow.

**

Betrayal

The cloud betrays itself
  By its shadow on the ground.
The earth betrays itself
  By its curve on the moon.
The ship betrays itself
  By the ripples on the sound.
The spring betrays itself
  By the flowers full in bloom.

The brook betrays itself
  By the singing waters's flow.
Art betrays itself
  By the treasure's rarity.
The cold betrays itself
  By the falling of the snow.
The rich betray themselves
  By their gifts to charity.

The fall betrays itself
  By the color of the leaves.
The wind betrays itself
  By the clouds in the skies.
The years betray themselves
  By the rings in the trees.
Love betrays itself
  By the light in the eyes.

Beware

Beware
Of illusions — nothing's what it seems.
Beware
Of ends that justify the means.
Beware
Of allegations — all pretence.
Beware
Of action without consequence.
Beware
Of words that promise or implore.
Beware
Of evil creeping in the door.
Beware
Of faith masking honest doubt.
Beware
Of fear that locks all action out.
Beware
Of gods that falsify their will.
Beware
Of oaths that force a man to kill.
Beware
Of wolves decked out in skins of fleece.
Beware
Of gifts that emanate from Greece.

**

Body Language

Body tense, standing straight,
Hands alive, articulate.
  Eyebrows arched in surprise,
  Eyelids hooded in disguise.

Bulging neck, corded taut,
Anguished anger onward brought.
  Chin in weakness forward bent,
  Shoulders serious with intent.

Stand-up hair, clothed in fear,
Bubbling voice, awash in cheer.
  Cheeks a-flush, ears aflame,
  Show the hidden shame.

Open mouth — disbelief,
Muscles slack — great relief.
  Thumbs down, in rejection,
  Sudden frown of dejection.

The body's full of words,
Adjectives, nouns and verbs.
  The body hides, the body seeks,
  The body hears, the body speaks.

Chaos

Behold, the human brain
Is very like a hurricane,

Mysterious, exotic,
Mathematically chaotic.

The brain at rest behaves.
Excited, streams of alpha waves

Act like jumping jacks,
Become dynamically complex,

Unpredictable,
Erratic and susceptible.

Chaos, in this sense,
Covers areas immense,

But within its border
Lies a deeply hidden order,

Simple little patterns
Within multitudes of atoms,

Or somewhere underneath,
Providing logical relief.

Neurons by the billions
Perform intricate cotillions.

Nonlinear dynamics
Is a kind of electronics —

Electron commuters
Associated with computers.

Systems found in nature
Predominately feature

Cycles, never lines
Of the strictly rigid kind.

Accurate prediction
Of the weather is a fiction.

It simply can't be done.
Weather happens to be one

Of the most non-
Linear items on

Nature's endless list
Of systems that exist.

Minor variations
In complex equations

Produce behavior that
Wildly upsets the *stat-*

Us quo — which inhibits
WX prediction, but exhibits

New bottom lines:
To wit, Chaos refines

Biology, and now
Is sorely needed to allow

The heart to operate
In health, and to facilitate

Knowledge of the main
Functions of the human brain.

Now we must abandon
The classic concept of Random,

In favor of Chaos,
Which affects all of us.

The theory of life —
Speculation now is rife—

Has to be rethought,
Since Chaos is fraught

With revolutionary
Concepts that vary,

In every direction,
With Natural Selection!

**

Coincidence

I never did,
No, never did,
Believe in coincidence.

I never could,
No, never could,
Conceive of such an inference.

I did not know,
I could not know,
The underlying truth.

It was too hidden,
Too deeply hidden,
Almost invisible, forsooth.

But now, at last,
At long, long last,
I've caught nature's drift.

The universe itself,
Yes, the universe,
Proclaims coincidence a myth!

Consensus

Consensus is — I can't keep mum —
Not the place the poet starts.
The whole, they know, is not the sum
Or the total of the parts.

To the cultural wind
The critic holds a wetted finger,
Hoping he or she can find
A better painter, sculptor, singer.

Politics by consensus
Now is all the rage.
Pollsters try to convince us
To believe the printed page.

Everybody seems to love
The one who looks a winner.
They push and pull and shove
To eat a hundred-dollar dinner.

I think that it's a shame
To only go where others lead.
Consensus is the game
Of a very slender reed.

Curiosity

Curiosity
Is the magic spark
That sets the mind afire,
The hand upon the lyre,
The seed that spells desire.

Curiosity
Is the unremitting search
For the truth within reality,
For the great within society,
For the one within variety.

Curiosity
Is the fountain of the arts,
The ounce of prevention,
The clue to intention,
The mother of invention.

Curiosity
Is the microscope
Of science and research,
Of philosophy, the perch,
Of morality, the church.

Declarations

The cock
Declares the night is done,
The wire
Declares the race is run.

The clouds
Declare that rain is near,
The birds
Declare that spring is here.

The banks
Declare the river's course,
The dam
Declares the power's source.

The moon
Declares the sun is high,
The wind
Declares that winter's nigh.

The sand
Declares the seas recede,
The dawn
Declares the light is freed.

The clock
Declares that time has passed,
This line
Declares the end at last!

Design

Sun and clouds
Design the evening sky.
Rain and soil
Design the corn and rye.

Moon and stars
Design the face of night.
Fires below
Design the mountain's height.

Wind and water
Design the canyon walls.
Rock and cliffs
Design the water falls.

Tooth and claw
Design the lion's meal.
Hand and heart
Design the potter's wheel.

Genes and DNA
Design the master plan.
Pride and greed
Design the mind of man.

Details

Details
Have never been my first
    Concern. My childhood day
    Was all too full, it seems,
    With normal childhood play.

Details
Arrived in middle school,
    They took me by surprise,
    They came in massive numbers,
    In every shape and size.

It took
A couple years or more —
    A long-term, shakedown cruise.
    Details were everywhere,
    I had to pick and choose.

The battle
Never seemed to end —
    Engagements every day.
    At last I comprehend:
    Details are here to stay!

Science
Was the field in which
    The horse at last was shod.
    In every discipline,
    Details — you see — were god!

Did You Know?
And Can You Tell Me Why?

I'm sure that you're aware
  Of this and that and those,
But did you know the almond
  Is related to the rose?

I'm convinced your mind
  Is very, very fertile,
But did you know the dinosaur
  Is younger than the turtle?

I know that you are smart,
  Just as smart as you can be,
But did you know about the storms
  At the bottom of the sea?

Is your physics up to date?
  Do you know how light behaves?
That particles — observed —
  Turn into waves?

I know you're clever, judging from
  The company you keep,
But do you know the meaning
  Of the quantum leap?

I know you're very calm,
  You're not afraid of thunder,
But did you know that Heaven
  Is another word for Wonder?

I know you're bright as day,
  And always right as rain.
But can you tell me why
  Life's so full of pain?

I know you're self-sufficient,
   You're the captain of your soul.
But can you tell me why
   We can never keep control?

Does?

Does the hill go up or down?
Does the mirror give or take?
Does the rope bend or break?
Does the gargoyle smile or frown?

Does the sun rise or set?
Does the ship sail or dock?
Does the music roll or rock?
Does the memory forget?

Does the water rise or fall?
Does the wind come or go?
Does the flower fade or grow?
Does the tree stand short or tall?

Does the shadow lead or follow?
Does the road begin or end?
Does the foe fight the friend?
Does the empty fill the hollow?

Dreams

The dreams that come by day
Swiftly fade away.
The dreams that darkness brings
Are strange, unlovely things!

I could write a book,
But I choose to overlook
The very worst examples.
Herewith some better samples:

Roads are hard to find,
Alleys always blind.
I suffer from angina,
Miss my plane to China.

Fruit trees die of frost,
Luggage turns up lost.
Resources always fail
When everything's on sale.

Cakes tend to fall,
Paint smears the wall.
I catch a falling star,
The sparkles turn to tar!

The Fallacy Of Logic

Let us praise persuasive logic —
    O, closely calculate!
Let us cleanse our hearts of panic,
    Doubts exterminate.

Let us plot our course with care,
    Rule out unruly chance.
Let dull devotion do its share,
    Eliminate romance.

Let us chart each consequence,
    Passion's out of season.
Let us increase intelligence,
    Revive reluctant reason.

When we've accomplished all our goals,
    When all is said and done,
We've saved our dull and savant souls,
    With not a trace of fun!

Fear

I feared to ask what the clouds meant,
For fear the clouds meant
Rain.
I feared to ask what the heart felt,
For fear the heart felt
Pain.

I feared to ask where the fire goes,
For fear the fire goes
Out.
I feared to ask what faith is,
For fear that faith is
Doubt.

I feared to ask where space ends,
For fear that space ends
Here.
I feared to ask what life means,
For fear that life means
Fear.

**

Fictionized

Distances are fictionized
    When the rain is very fine.
Empty space is fictionized
    When the stars brightly shine.

Beauty's often fictionized
    In the viewer's eye.
Hunger's often fictionized
    In the baby's cry.

History, too, is fictionized
    When we regard the past.
Art itself is fictionized
    When recognized at last.

The future's subtly fictionized
    By writers here and there.
Reality, too, is fictionized
    To everyone's despair.

I myself was fictionized
    In my mother's mind.
Everyone is fictionized,
    Each by his own kind.

**

Fortune

Fortune
Is a very fickle thing.
  Its giddy wheel may turn
  Your way before the day
  Expires, or may again
Simply face the other way.

Fortune
Is ambiguous and odd,
  Blind, without a doubt,
  Though not invisible.
  Its other name is Chance,
Equally quizzical.

Fortune
May be queen or may be king,
  May exist or not.
  It glitters bright as glass,
  But nothing shows,
And shatters when you pass.

Fortune
Stands for riches and for wealth.
  Both of which you make
  Or lose with equal ease.
  Fortune smiles, or fortune frowns,
Always pretends to please.

Fortunes
Can be read in the lines
  Traced upon our palms,
  In the auras above and between us.
  It is said of the planets,
The best are Jupiter and Venus.

**

The Future

There's a code you must break,
    There's a key you must find,
To avoid the mistake
    Of living like the blind.

There's a puzzle you must solve,
    A secret to unlock,
Unless you wish to revolve
    Like the hands of a clock.

There's mystery that holds
    The truth like a hostage,
There's a curtain in whose folds
    Lurks a hidden message.

Puzzle, code, secret, key —
    All lie deeply hidden
in Future Time, that we,
    To know, are forbidden.

But there is One high above,
    One who holds the Lightning Rod,
One whose name is Father, Love,
    Buddah, Allah, Jesus, God.

Gambling

I have a tendency to ramble,
Though I always say I shan't,
But I can't — I simply can't —
Resist the urge to gamble!

The time, it seems, is always right,
The game is never out of season,
Though it doesn't stand to reason
To sit and gamble every night.

Not every game suits my fancy —
While I love to roll the dice,
Playing cards seems a vice,
And roulette's much too chancy.

I may be wrong, I may be right,
I will hold nothing back,
The place to be is at the track,
Go at noon, stay till night.

Play the odds, I've heard it said,
Watch the numbers on the tote,
Every wager is a vote
For the best thoroughbred.

Be the day gray or sunny,
Place your bet, have your fun,
You will always get a run
For your money!

Like I said, I tend to ramble,
But remember all the same,
Life itself is just a game,
Every day is a gamble!

The Great Magician

Reality is a box of tricks
Which the mind plays upon us all,
'Tis but a room filled with mirrors,
With neither seam nor wall.

The moon at night does not appear
Till the sun sheds its light.
The stars cannot be found
Till dark possesses all the night.

The winds, indeed, though quite invisible,
Are powerful and free.
The vault of sky is empty nothingness
Till clouds arise from the sea.

Like shadows, dreams are thin and fleeting,
They come at night and then are gone,
Very like the dark,
They disappear with the dawn.

The Mind of Man is The Great Magician,
Hearth and home of every mystery.
Man and Nature — fact and fiction both —
Images and myth compose our history!

Greed

Greed is a deadly sin,
  As are gluttony and lust.
At first you seem to win,
  But the end is common dust.

Greed is not confined
  To lawless money lenders.
One should not be blind
  To the practices of vendors.

The sellers of manure back in old New York,
  Where the hymn of greed is sung,
Used sawdust, dirt and cork
  To adulterate the dung.

Wall Street is the place
  Where the instinct is inborn.
Like sheep the people race
  To be rounded up and shorn.

**

Happiness

Happiness
Is not in multitudes of friends,
But in a few of quality and worth.

Happiness
Is the sum of what we use
Of that bestowed on us at birth.

Happiness
Is choosing where to work and when,
Avoiding grief and strife.

Happiness
Is excitement and delight,
The jewels crowning fruitful life.

Happiness
Is taking care in unimportant things,
Accepting challenge unafraid.

Happiness
Is a kiss, a smile, a compliment,
A long forgotten kindness paid.

Happiness
We make and measure in ourselves,
Gladly to enjoy and share.

Happiness
Is like the wine from the grape,
A wine as sweet as it is rare.

**

Happiness Is Just Around The Corner

Mankind lives by myths,
  A fact of life with which
All mankind reckons,
  And the greatest of all myths,
The one that cuts like a switch,
  And yet forever beckons,
Is that happiness, like success,
  Is just around the corner.

But there is a truth,
  A truth, we must confess,
That has been forever:
  Happiness, like success,
Is *not* just around the corner;
  Happiness is now — or never.

Heaven And Hell

Heaven
Is a meadow wearing
April's coat of flowers.

Hell
Is a sudden hurricane
On top of April showers.

Heaven
Is a house built
Of May's apple blossoms.

Hell
Is a pernicious pack
Of petrifying possums.

Heaven
Is a house upon
A calm suburban street.

Hell
Is being trapped
In a jungle of concrete.

Heaven
Is happiness in love,
As decreed by fate.

Hell
Is when that fateful love
Turns to cruel hate.

Heaven
Is a hungry night
That feeds upon the stars.

Hell
Is insatiable,
Engulfing man in wars.

Heaven
Is perfect peace of mind,
And a conscience clear.

Hell
Is constant subterfuge,
And nights awash in fear.

Heaven
Is arriving at
A crystal clear conclusion.

Hell
Is immersion in
Absolute confusion.

Heaven
Is the magic key
To wishes and to dreams.

Hell
Is pain heaped upon
Trouble's swollen streams.

Heaven
Is undeserved mercy
That falls like gentle rain.

Hell
Is the endless struggle
For earth's worthless gain.

Heaven
Is moderation in
Everything you do.

Hell
Is the product of
Consuming evil's brew.

Heaven
Is moonlight sweet upon
The hillside's mossy bank.

Hell
Is dry and rocky soil
On the mountain's flank.

Heaven
Is the Here and Now,
The future's far away.

Hell
Is the endless wait
For the judgment day.

History

My subject here today
May not, in fact, be fit
For a light foray
Into the awesome pit

Of the past, that is, of history.
But certainly I feel
That history is a mystery
Only time can reveal.

Everything depends, of course,
Upon your point of view,
And men are the source
Of millions, one or two.

History is, for some,
Bereft of explanations.
And it's not a bit of fun
Explicating complications.

There's a view far more pleasant:
That the light of history may
Illuminate the present,
And ease the traumas of today.

But let me end by saying,
While we learn from the past,
The present is displaying
New traumas just as vast.

**

Home

Home is the womb
  From which we spring.
Home is a tree
  With a high, rope swing.

Home is a sky
  That's blue and clear.
Home is a heart
  That's free of fear.

Home is a fence
  With an open gate.
Home is a hearth
  With a glowing grate.

Home is a door
  With a lock and a key.
Home is a place
  From which to flee.

Home is a view
  Both east and west.
Home is the place
  A child knows best.

**

Hormones

Hormones
Excite both brain and body,
  And stimulate the nerves,
  Produce secretions when
  We deplete reserves.

Secretions
Leap into the blood,
  Hurry to each gland,
  Regulate and shape,
  Diminish or expand.

A potent
Chemistry, hormones
  Are one of nature's ploys —
  Increasing population —
  Little girls and boys.

Hormones work
In very secret ways,
  Out of your control.
  They can restructure both
  Your body and your soul.

Hormones are
A powerful attraction —
  Nature is so clever —
  They insure that man
  Will propagate forever!

**

Hostage

Clouds hold as hostage
  The moon that rides the night,
  While the starry hosts above
  Flee in utter fright.

Darkness holds as hostage
  The light before the dawn,
  As the King holds the Castle
  And the Knight holds the Pawn.

Symbols hold as hostage
  The letters of the word,
  As the silence holds the sound
  Ere the sound itself is heard.

Man holds as hostage
  Any other man,
  As the Devil held the Angels
  Before Time began.

I Don't Know

Why do songbirds sing?
Why do church bells ring?
Why do babies cling?
Why do cats play with string?
    I don't know,
    I don't know!

Why do eagles soar?
Why do lions roar?
Why is work a chore?
Why do two and two make four?
    I don't know,
    I don't know!

Why do pumpers prime?
Why do climbers climb?
Why do actors mime?
Why do verses rhyme?
    I don't know,
    I don't know!

Why do pastors bless?
Why do women dress?
Why do girls caress?
Now I confess that I could guess,
    But I don't *know*,
    I simply *do not know*!

If

If life in truth is tension,
I must also mention,
I must emphasize
That other equal prize,
Howsoever be it brief,
Instantaneous relief!

If happiness is indirect,
As I do indeed suspect,
I must also add
That nothing is so sad
As waiting an eternity
For joy and serenity.

If consumption is conspicuous,
And that's indeed ridiculous,
I sort of feel an obligation
To institute a regulation
That forbids one to hoard
All the treasure one has stored.

If nothing in the firmament
Is really truly permanent,
I must pay a greeting
To the swift and fleeting,
I must praise to the skies
All that pulses as it dies.

I Must Not

There are thoughts I must not think,
    There are words I must not speak.
There are wines I must not drink,
    There are goals I must not seek.

There are deeds I must not dare,
    There are bids I must not make.
There are joys I must not share,
    There are gifts I must not take.

There are hills I must not climb,
    There are games I must not play.
There are pumps I must not prime,
    There are prayers I must not pray.

There are stones I must not throw,
    There are tears I must not cry.
There are plants I must not grow,
    There are deaths I must not die.

In Defense of Darwin

Long before the *Beagle*,
Charles and Fanny lay for perfect hours,
   Lay close, by berries
In the straw — talking, watching showers

   Of sun and stars.
In school in Edinburgh, Darwin slowly died,
   Inch by inch, no
Other person there to note the beetles classified.

   Then the famous voyage
Became a grand and intellectual adventure.
   The youth, by inference
From geology, discerned the origin, in Nature,

   Of coral atolls,
Never having seen a living specimen —
   Early evidence
His mind had mastered scientific regimen.

   'Origins' appeared, and
Darwin joined the glorious company of prophets
   And apostles. And yet,
Today, the wind of controversy shakes and buffets.

   Still a matter of
Discussion. Still moot, the cosmic question:
   Do organisms in
Reality evolve and live through natural selection?

   Do solar systems
Spring alive and burn like fire and glow,
   And stars condense,
And galaxies from utter nothing grow?

Does culture
Climb the lengthy ladder chain?
Do words evolve?
Do apes indeed from reptile-fishes rain?

Time and Change
Sweep across the Garden. Tree leaves
Tremble, oceans swell,
Mountains rise, lava flows, clay breathes.

A random base
Must surely lie beneath Nature's station.
A universal order
Must surely govern matter's slow mutation.

Every species
Must descend from a single ancestry,
Or else we are
The victims of a clever cosmic forgery.

And vertebrates
Must indeed from invertebrates evolve.
But one dividing
Cell miscopies; makes a puzzle none can solve.

Horses, moles and
Manatees share a suite of common features:
Hair and jawbone
And an ear unique from other creatures'.

Bits of bone
Are all one needs to put together
Every animal.
Firm the law: every fossil has a father.

Every organism
Carries cells with patterned genes.
And every cell
Announces what its structure means.

**

Inspiration

Wide awake at night,
Or deep in desperation,
Man awaits the light
Of bold inspiration.

Inspiration is the spark
That sets the mind afire.
Inspiration is the quark
Which scientists require.

Poets, too, are inspiration's heirs,
And every artist in the nation.
CEO's arrange affairs
Inspired by inspiration.

Half-immersed in thought,
Hoping for a revelation,
Often one is caught
By sudden inspiration!

**

I Offer No Apology

I offer no apology
  When I present
  The long and short of hi-technology,
  When I accent
  The hard and soft of plant biology.

Don't question my ability
  When I stress
  The long and short of legal liability,
  When I assess
  The hard and soft of human viability.

I admit my reliance,
  Day in, day out,
  On the long and short of man's defiance,
  And I never doubt
  The hard and soft of computer science.

I show no petulance
  When I espy
  The long and short of locked-in excellence,
  Or descry
  The hard and soft of female preference.

I offer no apology
  When I report
  The long and short of earth's chronology,
  When I support
  The hard and soft of meaningful ontology.

It Cannot Be Learned

Love that's sweet is like a rose,
It cannot be learned.
Luck that's good comes and goes,
It cannot be learned.

Hope that's pure is like the light,
It cannot be learned.
Grief that's deep is simply right,
It cannot be learned.

A heart that's full is like the moon,
It cannot be learned.
Charm is like the sun at noon,
It cannot be learned.

Faith that's true is like a star,
It cannot be learned.
Life's a gift from afar,
It cannot be learned.

The Judgment Day

Each passing moment masks the guilt
Incurred each passing day.
Each birth begins the certain wilt
Imposed by nature's way.

Hist'ry crowds us from behind,
Already fate unfolds
The destiny that's pre-outlined,
Of all our future holds.

Man's feet have always been of clay,
He cannot keep a vow.
Look not ahead to judgment day,
The judgment day is now.

**

Just How Much Does An Oak Tree Know?

Just how much does an oak tree know?
  More than I, more than I.

Just how much does a white cloud weigh?
  Less than air, less than air.

Just how far can a river flow?
  As a bird can fly, as a bird can fly.

Just how long can an eagle stay?
  Long up there, long up there.

Just how far can a lighthouse look?
  Out to sea, out to sea.

Just how far can a baby crawl?
  Far away, far away.

Just how free is a babbling brook?
  More than me, more than me.

Just how far can a shadow fall?
  As light can play, as light can play.

Laughter

There is laughter full of joy,
There is laughter otherwise:
The laughter of survival,
The laughter of disguise.

There is raucous laughter,
There is laughter without sound.
There is laughter like a smile,
There is laughter like a frown.

There is laughter full of hope,
There is laughter tight with greed.
There is laughter *sans* a care,
There is laughter fraught with need.

There is laughter soft and sweet,
There is laughter loud and clear.
There is laughter when we greet,
There is laughter wrapped in fear.

There is laughter everywhere,
Morning, noon and night.
There is laughter in the dark,
There is laughter in the light.

**

Laughter — 2

Friendships oft begin
With laughter and with joy.
Laughter is the ploy
That brings a baby's grin.

Laugh and other folks
Laugh along with you,
Contagious, it is true,
And so are smiles and jokes.

Two things are worth the win:
The first is laughter and the other
Is the love of friend or brother.
Neglect's the cardinal sin!

Laughter's good for healing,
Or so it has been said:
Both the heart and the head
Share the happy feeling.

Please take my words to heart,
Laughing is no laughing matter
When you stop to consider
How soon the laughless do depart.

**

Life

A poem
Is a picture of the truth.
The truth
Is the mountain's solid core.
The core
Is beauty's wisdom tooth.
Beauty
Is the sun shining on the shore.

Love
Is a tree growing in a garden.
'A garden
Is a river running south.'
South
Is life without a warden.
Life
Is a city at the river's mouth.

**

Lighter Than A Breath

A maid's sweet sigh,
A wink of an eye,
    Lighter than a breath.

The touch of a ghost,
The shadow of a post,
    Lighter than a breath.

A heart that is true,
A love that is new,
    Lighter than a breath.

The whisper of love,
The feather of a dove,
    Lighter than a breath.

A bird's egg shell,
A magic spell,
    Lighter than a breath.

The thread of a seam,
The end of a dream,
    Lighter than a breath.

A baby's lisp,
A will 'o the wisp,
    Lighter than a breath.

The glance of a girl,
The glow of a pearl,
    Lighter than a breath.

**

Lost In The Computer

Anyone or thing can blunder,
But this you can't refute:
When you lose your name and number,
Nothing will compute!

Said the chap at Triple-A,
When I chose my route,
'I've got your route and number,
But your route and number
Simply won't compute!'

I went to give my blood,
Wearing my best suit.
Said the nurse, 'I've got your type and number,
But your type and number
Simply won't compute!'

Said the girl at the bank,
Who was very, very cute,
'I've got your name and number,
But your name and number
Simply won't compute!'

Said the airline clerk,
Looking quite astute,
'I've got your name and number,
But your name and number
Simply won't compute!'

Love

Like the sun,
Love shines forever bright.
Like the stars,
Love illuminates the night.

Like friends,
Love fills an empty room.
Like spring,
Love leaps from bud to bloom.

Like time,
Love lies within eternity.
Like space,
Love stretches to infinity.

Like knowledge,
Love confirms identity.
Like a poem,
Love outspans reality.

Like memory,
Love recalls the past.
Like laughter,
Love cements friendship fast.

Like courage,
Love overcometh strife.
Like mystery,
Love's as deep as life.

**

A Miracle

Every beat of your heart,
Every stop, every start
Is a miracle.

Every step that you take,
Every move that you make
Is a miracle.

Every thought in your mind,
Every word that you find
Is a miracle.

Every blink of your eye,
Every swallow, every sigh
Is a miracle.

Every touch of your hand,
Every organ, every gland
Is a miracle.

Every dollar that you earn,
Every fact that you learn
Is a miracle.

Every gift that you give,
Every moment that you live
Is a miracle.

Miracles

Music, when soft voices sing,
   Is a miracle.
Love, when two people cling,
   Is a miracle.

A poem, when it moves on magic feet,
   Is a miracle.
Happiness, 'though incomplete,
   Is a miracle.

Beauty, when the heart leaps up,
   Is a miracle.
Art, when it's not abrupt,
   Is a miracle.

Stars, when the night is young,
   Are a miracle.
Words, when spritely strung,
   Are a miracle.

A girl, who in beauty glides,
   Is a miracle.
The moon, tugging at the tides,
   Is a miracle.

Truth, when it shows its face,
   Is a miracle.
God's freely given grace
   Is a miracle.

**

Moderation

Hesiod said,
'Observe moderation,'
Seven hundred years before
The Virgin Mary bore
The Christ of our salvation.

Theognis
Could not allow the theme to rest,
Spoke to the circle of his fellows,
'Be not,' he said, 'Be not too zealous,
In all things moderation's best.'

Euripides,
Best writer of the Seven,
Spoke of, 'Simple moderation,'
Without further explanation,
As 'The noblest gift of heaven.'

Plutarch,
To ancient wisdom homage pays,
'Accomplish ends and means
By avoiding all extremes,
Give moderation praise.'

Montaigne
Proclaimed it in his native French,
'The most moderate measure
Is the one to treasure.'
Another mark on the bench.

Disraeli,
That clever English fox,
Declared that, even in excess,
Moderation spells success,
A pleasant paradox.

**

The Moment When

Long before you and I
Had scaled the wall of birth,
Long before we'd stumbled
On the masonry of time,

    The moment when history
    Began its endless course,
    The moment when we learned
    Evil's bond to discovery,

The moment when storms loom
And winds lean against the clouds,
The moment when the sun goes down
And trees absorb their shadows.

    The moment when the moon appears
    To be the sun's imagination,
    The moment when a forest fire
    Scribbles out a stand of trees,

The moment when the rays of stars
Tangle in mistletoe and ivy,
The moment when nature builds
Citadels of gravity and gilt.

    The moment when the artist
    Falls in love with magic light,
    And, at last, the moment when
    Fear and death take flight.

Money

Money is power,
    And power is money,
        And ever the twain shall meet.

Money is status,
    And status is money,
        Grovelling at your feet.

Money is love,
    And love is money,
        And evil's at the root.

Money is joy,
    And joy is money
        When you are in pursuit.

Money is trade,
    And trade is money,
        Where East conjoins with West.

Money is wealth,
    And wealth is money,
        The rich are most impressed.

Money is oil,
    And oil is money,
        Far beneath the earth.

Money is land,
    And land is money,
        Increasing your net worth.

**

More

More than lips,
Eyes govern a smile.
More than mother,
Peers govern a child.

More than fate,
Genes govern a man.
More than hands,
Winds govern a fan.

More than air,
Songs govern a bird.
More than breath,
Thoughts govern a word.

More than eyes,
Lips govern a kiss,
More than order,
Chance governs this!

Mystery

Beauty wears mystery's clothes,
Whisps of silk whisper secrets,
Hat and gloves carry codes
That have yet to be broken.

Art arrays itself in light and shadow,
Line and form are veiled in mist,
Meaning lies often fallow,
Words remain unspoken.

Science ever probes the unseen
Depths — the home of mystery —
With mind as sharp and eye as keen
As humans can create.

Wealth itself derives from sources
No one can comprehend.
The world itself is run by forces
Which are derived from fate.

Love's roots grow deep
Within a fertile soil,
Where all life's secrets sleep,
And every seed derives.

This universe wherein we live
Is wrapped in mystery.
We search for clues to give
Meaning to our lives.

**

NEW ABCs

Although it may seem absurd,
Avoid is the A-word
I aspire to articulate.
Avoid — this I strongly advocate —
Accidents and anxiety,
Avoirdupois and asperity.

It's a burden all must bear,
The baleful B-word called *Beware*.
Yet it bids us not to stray:
Beware of those who may betray,
Beware of bulls and things that creep,
Beware of wolves in clothes of sheep.

The C-word celebrates the Good Life,
First by circumventing strife,
Carefully avoiding perplexity and harm,
Emphasizing comfort, complexity and charm
C-words bring the Good Life near:
Consolation, character and cheer!

**

The New Reality

Man's nature is disorderly —
Science says it's true,
According to discoveries
Long overdue.

If disorder is his nature,
Can we then assess
Any single trait or feature
More orderly or *less*?

Physical duality
Applies to all mankind,
Which limits our ability
Precisely to define.

Wisdom that's conventional
Continues to insist
That every-day reality
Really *does* exist.

But science in the quantum phase
Says the very act
Of observation disarrays
And alters every fact.

So now appears a paradox,
Which everything explains.
While it reels from the shock,
Reality remains!

**

Niche Is In

I am happy to report
A change in our economy:
'Long' runs now are 'short' —
'Super star' in our astronomy.

> The trend today is to switch,
> 'Customizing' is preferred.
> 'Mass' is out, in is 'niche',
> Not a payment is deferred.

'Select' today is par,
'Designer' is the clue:
Build a better car
For the chosen few.

> Men are taller, girls are cuter,
> Better diet, better health,
> Thanks to the computer,
> For a new and better wealth.

Transactions are by wire,
Paper checks are obsolete,
Old systems soon expire,
Banks admit defeat.

**

Now, Go, My Love

Now go, my love, and catch a dream,
Now climb the highest mountain peak.
Remember, things aren't what they seem,
However long or hard you seek.

Now teach yourself to play or sing,
Become the envy of your peers.
But never trust the smallest thing
That strikes your eyes or e'en your ears.

But if you're born with special sight,
And if it truly is your fate,
You'll come into your every right,
You'll find it soon, or find it late.

Now go, my love, and live your life,
Traverse your road without a fear,
Hold high your head, endure the strife,
Your goal is good, the outcome clear.

Now go, my love, what e'er betide,
Prepare your soul for timeless sleep.
Live full your days, in God abide,
For God His promises will keep.

**

Not Too Greedy

Although I'm poor and I'm needy,
I would not be too greedy,
And I would not implore —
As I once did before —
That you part, without measure,
From a part of your treasure,
That you heap upon my head,
All the silver, all the bread,
All the manna from your heaven,
Be it risen or unleavened.

I'll admit, I do declare,
That I'd simply love to share
What came out not by pluck,
Not by work, but by luck,
Not that I do deserve
To deplete your reserve,
For I never have believed
You'd be hurt if relieved
Of a very small part
Of what's closest to your heart!

One With The Other

Though love and liberty
Are as sister is to brother,
They're not always compatible
One with the other.

Though law and justice
Are in marriage tied together,
They're never ever equal
One with the other.

Though hopes and dreams
Are subtle siblings forever,
They're not always in step
One with the other.

Though nature and reality
Come from common stock,
They're not equal by necessity,
One with the other.

Though peace and democracy
Are robot relatives,
They're not often in harmony
One with the other.

Though cause and effect
Appear to follow one another,
They're constantly in conflict
One with the other.

Order

Acts,
Perfectly predicted,
Have happened long before.

Things,
Accurately assembled,
Close creation's door.

Love,
Too long anticipated,
Seems ever less, never more.

Poems,
Too cleverly crafted,
Become a beastly chore.

Out Of Reach

The stars,
In all their luminescent glory,
Except by telescope and story:
Out of reach.

Happiness,
Despite our hopes and yearning,
Lies far beyond our ken and learning:
Out of reach.

Perfection,
For all its natural allure,
Remains forever pure:
Out of reach.

Success,
Though forever close, remains aloof,
Evades reason, rhyme and proof:
Out of reach.

Understanding,
Urged by pundits one and all,
Hovers just beyond the wall:
Out of reach.

Honor,
By all so much desired,
Too much required:
Out of reach.

Paradoxes

'Sunlight and shadow are the same,'
Mind and body share a name,
Pride is very clearly shame.

Courage is a name for fear,
The commonplace is often queer,
True and false alike appear.

Good and evil siblings are,
Near is very close to far,
Hole-in-one equals par.

Stupid is a twin to clever,
Joining often means to sever,
The instant is forever.

Heaven is to Hell adjacent,
Elderly is really nascent,
Every doctor is a patient.

A stranger often is a friend,
Come hither means to send,
Each beginning is an end.

**

Paradoxes — 2

On nothing, something firmly stands,
    Order has a random base,
Contraction suddenly expands,
    Neutrons fill empty space.

Simple often turns complex,
    History claims to be prediction,
Firmness really is pretext,
    Doubt becomes conviction.

Common turns to exotic,
    Fantasy is truly real,
Freedom seems to be despotic,
    Prose has poetry's appeal.

Nature looks artificial,
    What is is sometimes not,
Permanence is transitional,
    Remembrance often is forgot.

**

The Paradox Of Vanity

Ecclesiastes said,
    'Vanity of vanities; all is vanity.'
But not to be misled,
    Hold on to reason and to sanity.

Quite often you will find,
    To evil goodness must defer,
But vanity in humankind
    Is also virtue's spur.

Consider our too-human lot,
    How poor the mind would be,
Without the needle-shot
    Of heedless vanity!

Was ever there a beauty
    Who was not very vain?
But who would give up beauty
    To justify the plain?

No results we often see,
    In spite of earnest toil.
Perchance we'll find that vanity
    Provides a fertile soil.

The modest and the vain — they love
    To compete in prose and verse.
When push comes to shove,
    The vain finish first!

**

The Passing Of Remoteness

Once upon a time,
Years and years and years ago,
There were places far from home,
Where one could be quite alone,
Places famous for their remoteness.

There were places with romantic names,
Places deep in hidden valleys,
Places strange and exotic,
Often in the South Pacific,
Places known for remoteness.

Then we dreamed of taking journeys,
Reserving rooms in island villas,
Walking on foreign sands,
Dining in foreign lands,
Enjoying their remoteness.

But as today the world contracts,
As all things grow and connect,
Suddenly one bright day,
We awake and we say,
'We regret the passing of remoteness.'

People

People say that people are
    Creation's oddest creatures.
People say that people have
    The very oddest features.

In *other* people, most people
    Have no interest,
Unless those other people have
    An interest in them.

People always seem to think
    That *they* should stand to profit
From the foolish folly of
    Those who cannot stop it.

People always flatter people
    Who hold the reins of power,
Or those who are celebrities,
    If only for an hour.

People try very hard —
    They try so hard they strain —
To *understand* other people,
    But it's all in vain.

People watch other people
    When disasters strike.
Sorrow rarely touches them:
    They take perverse delight!

Pleasure

'There is pleasure in the pathless woods,'
In the lily and the rose,
Pleasure in the night,
Pleasure in repose.

There is pleasure in the loving heart,
Pleasure in the giving of a gift,
Pleasure in the new-born day,
In the healing of a rift.

There is pleasure in accomplishment,
Pleasure in a task well done,
Pleasure in the running of a race,
When the race is won.

There is pleasure in a smile,
Pleasure in the twinkle of an eye,
There is pleasure in a welcome,
Pleasure when the sun is high.

There is pleasure in a friend,
Pleasure in a modicum of wealth,
Pleasure in solitude,
Pleasure in great good health.

There is pleasure in discovery,
In the finding of a truth,
Pleasure in a sound night's sleep,
In the vigour of youth.

**

Power

The drive for power is the lot
Of every — well, *almost* every man,
For men connive and plot
Till power's in their hands.

Note that it was the desire
For power that caused the Angel's fall
From Heaven's heights to the fire
That engulfs one and all.

The man who rises to the heights
Of power quickly learns
That his soaring flights
Have imposed a host of awkward terms.

When riches vanquish poverty,
And fame has come his way,
He's lost his vaunted liberty,
And fear comes in to stay.

Power unlimited corrupts
The mind, Wiliam Pitt declares.
And power absolute disrupts
All of men's affairs.

When Will combined with Power is,
And Energy abets the pair,
We know a poison flower is
A-blooming everywhere.

**

Problems

Ordinary
Problems are perhaps
　　The most important problems
　　That everybody has.

But
Ordinary problems
　　Aren't my most important problems,
　　I really must confess.

A really
Ordinary problem —
　　Or so I seem to find —
　　Really solves itself.

My
Most important problem,
　　My most *pressing* problem,
　　Is simply me myself!

**Prosperity
(The Long And Short of It)**

There are those who have a flair
　　For accumulating wealth.
But pundits all declare,
　　It's done by trickery and stealth.

Prosperity should fill your life with joy,
　　But the Bible's words are clear,
It also could destroy
　　With satiety and fear.

'Prosperity's the very bond of love' —
　　The Bard pleads his case.
It comes like mercy from above,
　　By Providential grace.

Friends crowd close around
　　When you win the money race,
But enemies abound
　　When fortune turns her face.

If you've lost the vigor of your youth,
　　And you can't get on your feet,
As You Like It has the truth —
　　The uses of adversity are sweet!

**

The Question Of Ownership

I bought a parcel of land
That spans a summit of hill
And has a lovely stand
Of woods that daily spill

Their shadows across the sun-lit
Grass beside the brook
With a mantle of light upon it —
A page from Nature's book.

I own the land and all
There on and all that grows
There in spring and fall.
But do I own the wind that blows

In the tops of the trees?
Do I own the morning dew
On the grass? The light that flees
The shade? And all that grew

Along the water's edge?
Do I own the song
Of the birds in the hedge?
Is it right or wrong

That I claim to own
The waters that run
By a meadow sown
With diamonds from the sun?

Do I own the radiant light
Of stars at even-tide?
Do I own the magic sight
Of eagles that glide

Upon the currents that rise
From my shaded hill?
Do I own the cloud that flies
Above me? Do I fill

My heart for free with the notes
Of Nature's choir?
Do I own the myriad notes
That float in my own air?

I bought a parcel of land
And all that will upon it fit.
But where do I stand
On the question of ownership?

Reality

There are a thousand things that
Reality is, or is a part of,
But there also are,
In life's brief lexicon,
An endless list of things
Not real — in common language —
Yet more close to truth
Than touch-and-sight reality.

The first of these comes first in life,
When time is longer than
It later is,
And boy and girl
Are held, suspended, in the mists
Of childhood's magic, when innocence
Engulfs the heart,
And every dream is true.

**

Remembered

The sky is remembered light,
Music is remembered melody.
The dark is remembered night,
The play is remembered colloquy.

    The hour is remembered time,
    The house is remembered space.
    The poem is remembered rhyme,
    The smile is remembered grace.

Wisdon is remembered truth,
The comb is remembered honey.
Age is remembered youth,
Debt is remembered money.

    Decision is remembered choice,
    Man is remembered boy.
    Talk is remembered voice,
    Pleasure is remembered joy.

Riches, Fame And Pleasure

Wise Spinoza spared
No words when he declared
The things that most men treasure
Are Riches, Fame and Pleasure!

These three are dreams
Far beyond the means,
Far outside the ken,
Of most mortal men.

There are millions,
Very many millions
Of those who have played the game,
Who have won temporary fame.

Countless millions more
Paddle toward the shore
Of pleasure in a boat
They cannot keep afloat.

As for riches, sir,
Every man and cur
Would break his foolish neck
In order to deflect

A very large amount
Of money to his or her account.
Why is it that riches
Ever so bewitches

The likes of you and me,
As nectar to a bee?
The Bible and Koran
Declare that a man

Cannot wealth pursue,
Possessing virtue, too.
He richest is, in health,
Who's ignorant of wealth.

If you want a measure
Of riches, fame and pleasure,
You'll never make connection
Except by indirection!

Say What You Will

Say what you will,
    The lass herself misled me,
    Dreams of conquest fed me,
Say what you will.

Say what you will,
    All my friends deny me,
    Heaven's hosts decry me,
Say what you will.

Say what you will,
    Mournful bells alert me.
    Memories desert me.
Say what you will.

Say what you will,
    Aunts and uncles tease me,
    Only strangers please me,
Say what you will.

Say what you will,
    Cats and dogs offend me,
    Puffs of wind bend me,
Say what you will.

Say what you will,
    Facts tend to confuse me,
    Fiction may amuse me,
Say what you will.

Seeds

Gilt
Rubbed off the morning sun
Pollinates the clouds,
Giving rise to rain.

Silt
Within the ocean's waters
Seeds the oyster's pearls,
Nature's endless chain.

Wilt
Strikes everything and everyone,
Every fertile plant and flower,
Life begins again.

**

Silence

When the
Gates of day are closed,
  The gentle winds arise,
  As dusk descends, and bends
  The silence into sighs.

When politicians
End their perorations,
  And teachers cease to quiz,
  How very, very sweet
  The sound of silence is.

A paradox
Appears in nature, 'though
  Without the mind's compliance,
  The very cruellest lies
  Are often told in silence.

Sound
Can easily surpass
  The swiftest bird that flies.
  Sounds expire, and yet
  The silence never dies.

Silence is
As soft as mother's love,
  And surely lasts as long,
  And mothers say it is
  More musical than song.

I cannot list
All its many virtues,
  For silence, I am told,
  Is more malleable,
  More valuable than gold.

Silence is
A blessing from above.
It falleth like the dew,
The many don't approve,
But it satisfies the few.

**

Statistics

Statistics are a funny game —
Where funny means peculiar,
Where win and lose are just the same —
War alone is similar.

One to ten appear to be
The basic units utilized.
Plus and minus seemingly
Most easily computerized.

The problem is that figures lie,
Producing tons of doubt.
One thing there is one can't deny:
Garbage in, garbage out.

Though it's darkest 'fore the dawn,
A little light is shed, 'tis true.
Conclusions always can be drawn,
Depending on your point of view.

Tension

Tension is a strange
  But essential thing.
Tension is the force
  Within a coil of spring.

Tension lies within
  The very heart of life.
But tension oft conceals
  The secret cause of strife.

Tension can be good,
  A pleasure that abides.
But tension can be ill,
  A force that divides.

Tension is the wing
  That lifts one up in flight.
Tension is a source
  Of joy and delight.

Tension often is
  As hard as lava rocks.
Tension always is
  An odd paradox.

Things That Count

Once it was politics,
    Power and position.
Now it's cholesterol,
    Fiber and nutrition.

Once it was vision,
    Close to mankind's heart.
Now it's technology,
    Morality and art.

Once it was the science of
    Society and race.
Now it's astronomy,
    Cosmology and space.

Once it was fashion,
    Popularity and flair.
Now it's education,
    Poetry and prayer.

Once it was work,
    A twelve-hour day.
Now it's leisure time,
    Family and play.

Think Your Way

Truth,
It seems, is full of flaws,
When truth
Is sired by thought.

In truth,
You cannot *think* your way
To truth,
And truth *cannot* be bought.

Forsooth,
The same is true of every other thing:
In truth,
You cannot think your way to anything!

The path to truth,
We learn from history,
Like every other thing,
Is veiled in mystery.

**

Thoughts

I
The thoughts of youth are often deep,
Keeping dreams alive.
The thoughts of middle-age repeat,
And on occasion thrive.
Older thoughts are often short —
No honey in the hive.

II
Thoughts in fertile younger minds
Develop deeper roots.
Thoughts within the middle group
Favor hunting boots.
Senior's thought scatter out,
As a shotgun shoots.

III
Thoughts of youth come fresh and fast,
A leap to conclusion.
Middle thoughts are indirect,
Counting on profusion.
Thoughts in many older minds
Wander in confusion.

IV
Youthful thoughts lead to actions,
Impulsive though they be.
Middle thoughts are second thoughts,
Wiser, possibly.
Seniors stress reflective thoughts,
Closer to philosophy.

**

Three Things Most Needed Are

Three things most needed are,
To reach life's pinnacle,
Three things that remove the bar
To certain, sure success:
Stamina and courage
And good old-fashioned luck.

Three things most needed are
To reach the goal of love,
Three things love demands are:
Unselfish hands,
A lot of patience and
A heart that endlessly expands.

Three things most needed are
To reach the very top
In the finer arts:
Talent and persistence,
And originality,
All in equal parts.

Three things most needed are
In business and all else
Where risk is the chief ingredient:
Expertise, of course,
Lots of money and
Luck beyond belief!

**

Time

Time,
Encircled by eternity,
The void's earnest slave,
Burst its bonds
And leaped to life
When Space was born.

Time's
Press stamped out the hours,
Minted minutes,
Sliced the seconds,
Stringing to infinity
Its endless silver store.

Time
Encases itself in mantel clocks,
In courthouse cupolas,
In lady's lockets
And watches on the wrists of men,
And the towers of Big Ben.

**

The Tree Of Life

Rooted in the muck,
The Tree of Life has Man
On its tipmost top.

Before the climate yet was ripe
And spirit silently succumbed to
Gross materialism,

Darwin's firm opinion:
'Brain of child resembles parent stock.'
Twenty years too soon.

But slowly, natural selection
Became by faith and gradual evolution
The new religion.

Cuvier spoke its basic tenet:
'All ancient animals may be rebuilt
From bits of bone.'

Reptiles — fishes — apes —
Together form a fossil sequence.
Every fossil has a father.

Plain empirical truth —
Every living organism has a living parent.
A hundred million years.

And farther back in time,
No animals walked upon the earth,
But animals now abound.

By gradual evolution
Mammals from non-mammals came.
Logic spells it out: QED.

Square-faced scientists,
In white lab coats or blue work shirts,
Began the quiet rebellion.

Said the Tree of Life
Lives in men's minds by faith alone,
The fossil record runs to zero.

Vertebrates may not
From invertebrates evolve. No species
Comes from another.

From current craft,
'The concept of ancestry is not accessible.'
Only patterns can be read.

Evolution's agnostics
Find nature much too disorderly,
Turn to taxonomy.

Cladists challenge orthodoxy:
'Man knows nothing of the ancestry of man.'
A fossil is a mess on a rock.

Time and process are
The citadels of science — but there are
No connecting lines.

God's finger touched the void,
Transformed the universal muck, and
Brought the Tree to Life.

•

**

Truth

Pilot asked what truth is —
   Pilot's clever plot.

One can't truly say *what* truth is,
   Only what it's *not*.

Truth only may be wide,
   Narrow, it is not.

Truth can freely flow
   And never never clot.

Truth could be flexible,
   Rigid, it could not.

Truth may well be relative,
   Absolute, it's not.

•

**

Truth And Error

The controversy flares anew,
   Man the battle stations.
   The troops of truth are few,
Error's shine like constellations.

Crushed to earth, truth will rise
   To face the foe again.
   Clever error flies
Ahead, commands the victory train.

Error's age is ages old,
   Truth's forever young.
   Error's stout and bold,
The song of truth is shyly sung.

Truth disperses and divides,
   The people polarized.
   Error takes no sides,
Its lands already colonized.

Truths are very fragile flowers,
   They neither spin nor toil.
   Errors need no showers,
Grow in every kind of soil.

Truth plays a cautious hand,
   Gambling's not her game.
   Error's happy band
Considers all the odds the same.

Truth keeps the door ajar
   For quick recovery.
   Fearless errors are
The portals of discovery.

Errors bear a lovely fruit,
    Especially in science.
    Truth gets the boot
From everyone's experience.

When I review the battle field,
    Observing tooth and claw,
    Neither side will yield —
I proclaim the fight a draw!

**

Truth And Fiction

From the very start,
Let's make a clear distinction
'Twixt what is real and what is fiction:
Between the whole and the part.

Truth is commensurate
With the facts of reality,
For reality has the ability
To win this long debate.

Truth is always stranger
Than fiction can now or ever
Be, regardless of how clever
Is fiction's shrewd arranger.

Take a close look at nature,
Especially when it's tropical
And you're truly philosophical,
Is there truth in nomenclature?

In short, what's in a name?
A truly academic argument,
By which no harm is meant:
Are truth and fiction just the same?

Let us look a little deeper,
Far beneath the surface —
Remember, in a turf race,
The winner's oft a sleeper!

Fiction can reveal the truth,
For truth may be a paradox —
Clever like a fox,
As sly as vodka in vermouth.

But perhaps we never should allow
That either is deceptive —
The mind will not accept it —
The truth is better, anyhow!

**

Truth Is No Stranger

'Truth is no stranger'
  To falsehood and to fable.
The weak are no strangers
  To the strong and the able.

Science is no stranger
  To myth and to mystery.
The future is no stranger
  To the past of history.

Magic is no stranger
  To the simple and the clear.
Courage is no stranger
  To the heart full of fear.

Ice is no stranger
  To the heat of the fire.
The next is no stranger
  To the present and the prior.

The night is no stranger
  To the dawn and the dew.
The many are no stranger
  To the sparse and the few.

The sky is no stranger
  To the bottom of the sea.
The slave is no stranger
  To the master and the free.

**

Uniqueness

There is uniqueness everywhere,
Every flake of snow,
Every star aglow,
Every strand of human hair.

There is uniqueness all around,
Every image in the eye,
Every infant's tiny cry,
Every tone of every sound.

There is uniqueness up above,
Every summer cloud,
Every eagle proud,
Every sparrow, every dove.

There is uniqueness down below,
Every valley floor,
Every seed and spore,
Every fish and coral show.

There is uniqueness deep within,
Each and every part
Of every human heart,
Every hope, every sin.

There is uniqueness deeper still,
Every pain, every grief,
Every sigh of relief,
Every act of the will.

Variety

If
Variety
Is
The Spice
That
Makes
Life
Bubble,
I'm in trouble!

**

War

War instills a sense
  Of close community,
At the expense
  Of man's humanity.

War shows a face
  Of apprehensive good,
All without a trace
  Of true brotherhood.

War's heart is in power,
    In rational autonomy,
Bringing into flower
    The national economy.

War is a rehearsal
  Of tragedy to come,
Of evil universal,
    For each and every one.

War is at the heart
  Of the life of every man,
War is a part
  Of nature's master plan.

**

What Care I?

What care I where perils lie,
If only Fortune be not shy?

What care I how black the night,
If stars aloft are burning bright?

What care I how slow the dawn,
If the fears of dark are gone?

What care I how deep the snow,
If in spring the flowers grow?

What care I how sad the song,
If the song be not too long?

What care I how hot the sun,
If the summer's course is run?

What care I how pale the moon,
If harvest days are coming soon?

What care I how short the day,
If winter soon will fade away?

What Do You Do?

What do you do
When skies are blue
And so is Monday?

What do you do
When ship and crew
Refuse to work on Sunday?

What do you do
When the heat goes up the flue
And leaves you cold?

What do you do
When the bills are overdue,
And the tent's about to fold?

What do you do
When all that you accrue
Are ancient aches and pains?

What do you do
When company is due
And every day it rains?

What do you do
When clients start to sue
And everything unravels?

What do you do
When regret, remorse and rue
Permeate your travels?

What do you do
When friends are passing through
The airport late at night?

What do you do
When you plan and fret and stew,
And nothing comes out right?

What If By Chance?

What if by chance
    I'd search the sky at night
    And not a star appear?

What if by chance
    You'd leave my sight
    And fill my heart with fear?

What if by chance
    The seas should rise
    And overflow the shore?

What if by chance
    My garden dies
    And Eden is no more?

What if by chance
    A mighty cataclysm came,
    The earth consumed by fire?

What if by chance
    I could not explain
    My reluctance to expire?

What if by chance
    A miracle occurred
    And every soul was saved?

What if by chance
    Death could be deferred
    Until all debts were paid?

Why?

While so many things are free,
Like the leaves on the tree,
Like the bees and their honey,
Why must man work for money?

While nature gives us fruit,
Like the tuber, nut and root,
Like the seed, stem and bark,
Why must man slave till dark?

While the sun spills its treasure,
Like the light without measure,
Like the warmth in the west,
Why can't men ever rest?

While the sea sends its wealth,
Sends us all of itself,
Why must man have to pay
The Piper night and day?

Why, Oh, Why?

Why do birds so early sing?
Why do bees with honey sting?
Why do showers April bring?
Why does summer follow spring?
Why do bells at noontide ring?
Why do babes to mothers cling?

Why do three strikes count you out?
Why do boxers flaunt their clout?
Why does anger make one shout?
Why do good girls often pout?
Why are rich men often stout?
Why do sailboats come about?

Why do babes kick and cry?
Why do lovers always sigh?
Why do gossips have to pry?
Why do shoppers always buy?
Why do eagles fly so high?
Why, oh, why? Why, oh, why?

I think the reason is because —
Grammar's rules give me pause —
Nature follows strictest laws,
Sharks don't have the tightest jaws,
Beastly man's so full of flaws,
Women have the sharpest claws.

Windows

Knowledge is
A window wide upon the world,
   Admitting to the minds
   Of men a picture of
The past as slowly it unwinds.

The sun
Arises with reluctant dawn,
   Peering through the golden
   Window of the East,
No longer to the night beholden.

Astronauts
Depend upon a narrow window,
   As they begin the race
   To return safe and sound
From the vacuum of space.

In days
Of old, English public houses,
   With ale for one and all,
   Put lavender in the windows,
Ancient ballads on the wall.

Picture
Windows once were all the rage,
   In houses all about,
   Pictures looking in,
Better pictures looking out!

**

Wit

If
Brevity
Is
The
Soul
Of
Wit,
This is it!

**

Wonder

Wonder
Is the awe that strikes a child
When first it views the world,
And the times before it's hurled
Into the jungle wild.

Wonders
Are most amazing things,
Like Rhodes' great Colossus,
Artemis' Temple at Ephesus,
And man aloft on silver wings.

A smile
From the bright and beauteous eyes
Of a bright and beauteous girl
Is a wonder, like the curl
That on her head often lies.

Man,
'Tis said — and Darwin said it —
Is the wonder of the universe,
That very man who is the curse
And spoiler of the planet.

Wonder
Is worship's root and base,
Or so Carlyle declares,
And love with wonder pairs
To gild religion's face.

**

Words To The Wise

Never cut your conscience
    To fit the current fashion.
Never give your heart
    In a fit of passion.

Never fail to smile —
    It's a sign of elation.
Never fault a child,
    The soul of creation.

Never try to drive
    Much too hard a bargain.
Never keep alive
    Anger that is far gone.

Never cry too loud,
    Or be averse to contemplation.
Never be so proud
    As to forget your station.

PART V

MISCELLANY

A Gemstone Calendar

Garnet is the stone
  That two-faced Janus wears
  To start the year anew.
One face faces back,
  The other looks ahead,
  As all beginnings do.

The gem is amethyst —
  The month of expiation,
  Nemo placed it here.
By design the month
  Is short a day,
  To fit within the year.

The bloodstone comes of age
  Amid the winds of March.
  The vernal equinox
Celebrates the spring —
  Early daffodils,
  Peonies and phlox.

Diamond is the gem,
  Most precious of them all.
  But April is inconstancy!
So choose most carefully
  Your mate, and beware
  Of infidelity.

Emerald is the gem
  That introduces May,
  Month of early growth.
Lilies crowd the fields,
  And all the other flowers —
  Spring is nothing loath.

Pure and precious pearl
    Adorns the month of June,
    The middle of the year.
Bride and groom agree
    To speak the vows that
    Make the rice appear.

Now comes the ruby month,
    That warm and lengthy month,
    The seventh one in line.
Its name from Caesar comes,
    Whose toga once was stained
    As deep a red as wine.

Sardonyx is the gem,
    The lovely, layered stone
    That marks our number eight,
The most majestic month.
    Augustus was the Caesar
    Who met a Caesar's fate.

Sapphire's precious light
    Illuminates the month
    That Labor celebrates.
Students start to school,
    Vacation time is past,
    The job at work awaits.

Opal is the stone
    Of the magic month
    When I myself was born.
Harvest is the time —
    Wheat within the shock,
    Honey in the horn.

Topaz holds the honor
    Of that historic month
    When Winthrop sighted land.

The Pilgrims were the hosts,
    Serving native birds —
    The guests were Indian.

Turquoise's lovely light
    Marks the holy time
    Of precious Jesus's birth.
Since that inspired event
    Nothing stays the same
    Upon this planet earth.

**

A List of People I Have Never Known
But Maybe You Have

Charlton Heston, Gregory Peck,
James Thurber, E. B. White,
Charles MacArthur, Ben Hecht,
Paul Robeson, Richard Wright.

Thackeray and Charles Dickens,
Tennyson and Alfred Noyes,
C. S. Lewis and Stephen Hawking,
Bernard Shaw and James Joyce.

Doyle, Elizabeth and Bob,
Truman, Bess and Harry,
Charles and Linda Raab,
Brown, John and Jerry.

The Lady called Antonia,
Charles and Princess Di,
The Laird of Thistleonia,
And the late Christopher Fry.

A List of Things That Are Blue

Skies,
A baby's eyes,
Mountains far away,
And corn in New Mexico.

Lake Louise,
The shade of willow trees,
Waves off the beach at Waikiki,
And the high glacier's icy glow.

Quilts,
Jockey's silks,
Almost every Monday,
And a slice of the rainbow.

Scarves for women,
Pools for swimming,
Sewing thread, Texas bonnets,
And shadows in the river far below.

**

A List of Things That Are Soft

Thai silk,
Buttermilk,
Cream of wheat,
And the early winter's snow.

Cat's purr,
Rabbit's fur,
Swans' feathers,
And the blanket on the bunk below.

Sifted sand,
Sally Rand,
Cotton shorts and shirts,
And the gentle water's flow.

Camel's hair,
Puffs of air,
Fields of dandelions,
And the glances women throw.

**

A List Of Things That Catch The Light

Diamonds,
Copper kettles,
An early morning sky,
Cotton clouds flying by,
And the surface of a lake.

Hubcaps
And sequins,
Mirrors on the wall,
A swirling crystal ball,
And gemstones real or fake.

Silver coins
And glacial ice,
Snow upon a mountain top,
An aircraft's whirling prop,
And a very large vanilla shake.

Tin foil,
Steel beams,
A nurse's uniform,
Fields of wheat and corn,
And birthday candles on a cake.

Golf balls,
Windshields,
Balloons in upper air,
Twenty swans and a pair
Of mallard ducks and a drake.

A Toast

Here's to the girl with the bright blue eyes,
    With round, red cheeks,
    With a blouse that peeks,
Here's to the girl who softly sighs.

Here's to the lad with the light brown hair,
    With great good looks,
    With a thumb that crooks,
Here's to the lad whose face is fair.

Here's to the wife with the bright red dress,
    With no crows feet,
    With lips so sweet,
Here's to the wife the angels bless.

Here's to the man with the high forehead,
    With a mind that's keen,
    With a look serene,
Here's to the man with a son well-bred.

Here's to the babe with the dimpled smile,
    With a bottom soft,
    With feet aloft,
Here's to the babe with a low profile!

Braces

Fashions fluctuate
    At a rapid pace —
An expected trait
    Of the marketplace.

Dresses seem to be
    In motion every year,
Every line is free
    To fade and reappear.

In the better shops
    That carry things for men,
Braces are the tops,
    Returning yet again.

Braces, I avow,
    Once were called suspenders,
Once were out but now,
    Have numerous defenders.

Even farther back
    On fashion's calendar,
Following the track
    Of brace's harbinger,

We find that gallusses
    Were favored on the farm
By men with calluses,
    Or other signs of charm.

But now the current fad,
    Among the few who care,
Both for son and dad,
    Is to wear a pair

Of braces fixed to buttons,
   Solid-color braces,
Red if they are gluttons
   For the races.

If all else is normal,
   Blue or green at night,
Unless they're going formal,
   Which calls for black or white!

Coffee

Coffee
Is a subject of
   Concern to you and me.
   I trust this dissertation
   Will earn my PhD.

Coffee
Beans are mountain grown —
   Allow me to explain:
   All beans are mountain grown,
   Never on the plain.

Coffee
Beans are gathered by
   Careful human hands,
   Sorted, dried and sold
   In several different brands.

Experts
Say Jamaican Blue
   Mountain is the best,
   Kona's close behind,
   Then follow all the rest.

Supermarkets
Carry many cans
   Of coffee on the shelf,
   Or bins of beans
   You may grind yourself!

Cowboys

Fill ya coffee cup,
Settle down and listen up,
Let me tell ya how, boys,
Y'can become cowboys.

Get y'self a pair of boots,
And a gun that really shoots,
Get a pair-a silver spurs,
Leather chaps agin' th' burrs.

A brass buckle and a belt,
A roan horse already gelt.
Weather m'aint not be th' best
When y'ur headin' to th' west,

Find a river or a branch,
Ride th' wire to a ranch,
Sign y'ur name, learn th' ropes,
Ride th' range, hunt th' slopes,

Run a whole bale-a wire,
Gather wood, build a fire,
Wade th' deep water shoals,
Fry a fish over coals.

Settle back, watch th' moon,
Listen to th' dogies croon.
Flick a pick, sing a song,
As th' night lingers on.

Avoid th' tree's knobby roots,
Set y'ur pack, shed y'ur boots,
Sleep th' sleep of th' just,
Snore a bit, if y' must.

Rise at morn with th' sun,
Another day has begun.
So soon y'll learn th' trade,
So little y'll get paid!

The Dow

Every day at noon and five
I keep myself alive
    By calling up my broker.
I can't wait any longer,
My desire is even stronger
    Than when I'm playing poker.

Let me elucidate now:
When I refer to The Dow,
    It's not the company chemical,
My interest never springs
From such commonplace things,
    Pharmaceutical or medical.

I'm talking things substantial,
Monetary and financial.
    Are my stocks any higher?
On, yes, they're very blue,
And, like Topsy, they just grew.
    Should I take another flyer?

My heart really quakes
When the market swings and shakes
    On a quarter-million shares.
That's a lot of changing hands,
But it meets the demands
    Of a quarter-million squares!

Garage Sales

In the spring and in the fall,
Take a ride, have a ball.

Weekly papers advertise
Slacks and suits in every size.

Racks and racks of ladies' clothes,
Hats for heads, socks for toes.

Rakes and tools and garden hose,
Every kind of plant that grows.

Lots and lots of children's toys,
Skates and scooters, bikes for boys.

Sofas, chairs and bedroom suites,
Blouses plain and skirts with pleats.

Breakfast sets and coffee tables,
Rabbit furs and costly sables.

Sales like these often thrive
In the yard or on the drive.

Rent a table, take a slot
In the local parking lot.

But in all this barrage,
Whoever bought one garage?

Horse Racing

At the track,
When racing is in season,
Hopes rise to extremes,
For the very reason
The track is selling dreams.

At Saratoga,
You breakfast on the terrace,
Slender elms overhead,
The regal horses race
Every one a thoroughbred.

At Churchill Downs,
Skip the favourite, they say,
When the Roses Race is run.
Be sure to make your play
'Twixt 3- and 10-to-one.

On Long Island,
If you want to hit the mark,
There's money you can make,
Go to Belmont Park,
Play the odds, for heaven's sake!

At Hialeah,
Flamingoes are the thing
That get your attention,
But still you take a fling
At the thoroughbred convention.*

At Royal Ascot,
You'll never make a buck.
Horses aren't the passion,
You're simply out of luck
If you're out of fashion.

*Since this was written, racing has been phased out at Hialeah. Fans will miss it sorely, though most fared very poorly!
**

Lite

Lite crept in before we knew it,
      Took our house by storm.
'Though I totally eschew it,
      Lite became the norm.

I know, of course, that lite means light,
      But it goes against the grain.
While at first I tried to fight,
      It captured my domain.

Beer is lite, yogurt's lite,
      And so is cottage cheese.
But why does everyone delight
      In thinking everyone agrees?

Before you know it, chaos reigns.
      If every blight turns to blite,
Then losses counteract the gains,
      'Cause nothing's right unless it's rite.

I ask you now, should smite be smight?
      Or the other way around?
Go fly a kite, or is it kight?
      The reasoning is sound.

Memos

'Memo' stands for 'Memorandum'.
The plural, 'Memoranda',
Is used to expand a
List, or as a new addendum

To documents and notices.
Memos may be found,
Indeed, they abound,
In governmental offices,

And in larger businesses,
Not ot mention small,
Where memos cover all,
Or, at least, the major genuses

Of a multitude of subjects.
Announcing duty hours,
Remember to buy flowers,
Turn in estimates and budgets.

At home, memos by the score,
In crayon or in ink,
Above the kitchen sink,
On the fridge or freezer door.

Incidental memos most —
'I need money bad,'
'I love you, Mom and Dad,'
'Becky's back from the coast!'

One More

One kiss more, one tear less,
One carnivore under stress.
One maid more, one lad less,
No rapport, no duress.

> One day more, one night less,
> From your store, one caress.
> One fifth more, one pint less,
> Count to four, then confess.

One hand more, one trick less,
Deuces bore, aces bless.
One king more, one pawn less,
Two not four can play chess.

> One car more, one horse less,
> One on shore, one out west.
> One stroke more, one putt less,
> Ne'er before, such distress.

Stolen

The winds of spring abound with scents,
    Stolen from the flowers.
The fields are cool and dark with damp,
    Stolen from the showers.

The mirror moon has a golden glow,
    Stolen from the sun.
A poem's a picture filled with images,
    Stolen one by one!

**

Stretching

Stretching is,
You see, an automatic thing,
  A sort of reflex thing,
  That men and women do,
  And other creatures, too.

Cats, you know,
Are famous for their morning stretch,
  That satisfying stretch,
  When they awake from sleep,
  From oh, so stiff'ning sleep.

Dogs, perforce,
Are trained to chase, to run and leap
  For frisbees in their steep
  Descent from upper air,
  A feat beyond compare.

Horses are
Requested by their jockeys,
  In almost every race,
  To stretch their legs and necks,
  Augmenting owner's checks.

Money, too,
Is often asked to stretch and stretch,
  To pay the rent and fetch
  The bacon home before
  The lengthy month is o'er.

The Nightly News

It's all a game, a wondrous game,
A game I can't refuse,
Within a frame — oh, frightful frame! —
The TV Nightly News.

    Tom's on first, Dan's on second,
    Connie Chung's on third.
    Others, too, with whom to reckon,
    Feathers of a single bird.

More facts there are than one can count,
Though some, no doubt, are fiction.
I love to sip at the fount
Of Peter Jenning's diction.

    Diane pitches, Sammy catches,
    All with mixed emotions.
    Amid the ads I catch dispatches
    From across the oceans.

It's all a game, a wondrous game,
The channel I can choose.
It differs yet is all the same,
The TV Nightly News!

Too

Kindergarten

Too full of childhood wonder,
Too clean to play outside.
Too naive to ponder,
Too full of childish pride.
Too willing to expect,
Too afraid to speculate,
Too shy to object,
Too early to matriculate.

Middle School

Too young to drive a car,
Too slow at grammar and at math,
Too full of self by far,
Too quick to vent their wrath.
Too full of life to care,
Too inclined toward confusions,
Too selfish to be fair,
Too quick to jump to conclusions.

High School

Too hasty and too rude,
Too bold and cocksure,
Too fast for their own good,
Too careless to be pure,
Too inclined to start-and-stop,
Too occupied by looks,
Too prone to gossip and to plot,
Too cavalier of books.

Summer Camp

Too cool to ask advice,
    Too much in love with ease,
Too afraid of ticks and lice,
    Too self-concerned to please.
Too busy much to write,
    Too prone to trick and play,
Too macho not to fight,
    Too inclined to sleep half the day.

College

Too inclined to fraternize,
    Too slavish to hormones,
Too prone to socialize,
    Too long on telephones.
Too smart to study or to read,
    Too proud to bow and scrape,
Too much in love with speed,
    Too loving of escape.

Young, Upward and Mobile

Too clubby and too clannish,
    Too poor to buy a Jag,
Too much Anglo, too little Spanish,
    Too inclined to chew the rag.
Too much in love with comfort,
    Too steeply deep in debt,
Too dependent on support,
    Too quick to gamble and to bet.

Universal Questions

Do we really know
    How the universe behaves?
Is it made up, simply,
    Of particles or waves?

If Alpha equals '1' —
    Why does not Omega?
And why is every star
    Not as bright as Vega?

If truly we believe
    In Singularity,
Why are we so stunned
    By Irregularity?

How does the reversal
    Of pure gravitation
Bring about the thing
    That is called Inflation?

In the very first Three Minutes,
    Why is it that the photons
Critically outnumbered
    All the baryons?

Stars and planets are so round,
    Why, then, is it that
The smooth and whole universe
    Is so very, very flat?

When all else appears
    So very much *pro rata*,
Why is cosmology
    So starved of essential data?

Sun and moon differ so
    In size, can you tell me why
The sun and moon appear
    So equal in the sky?

I think I would explain this
    If I truly could —
Why does the royal sun
    Rotate slower than it should?

Why is dark matter missing —
    As well as other things?
What is supersymmetry?
    And what are superstrings?

Is not the universe
    Older than the earth?
How much, in our cosmology,
    Is a billion worth?

To the creation
    Of the universe,
The observer is essential,
    And so, it seems, is the reverse!

**

The Urban Hum

I can hardly find the words
To describe the urban hum.
No, it's not the birds
The sounds are coming from.

I hear it morning, noon and night,
That very strident noise,
From neighbours left and right,
Women, men and boys.

The urban hum combines the sounds
Of the edger and the mower,
And from all around
The leaf's raucous blower.

I love to see the sight
Of the lawn in manicure,
But who has the right
To sound-pollute the pure

Pellucid air around us?
Still, I'll admit I know
The urban hum has found us
And will not let us go.

Airport jets are just our luck,
Add the sirens of police,
EMS and the garbage truck —
Will we ever get relief

From the sum, the everlasting sum
Of the sounds of the urban hum?

To Verbal-ize

It should come as no surprise —
Though I shall fight it tooth and nail,
I suspect that I shall fail —
This tendency to verbalize.

Every single common noun,
And some that are not so,
The situation's got so,
It makes a man of grammar frown.

I'll accept a very few,
Like, well, prioritize.
But, hey, words like casualize
Are much too odd and new.

Oh, yes, indeed, I know that love
Is very often casualized,
And politics is strategized,
But that is no excuse, by Jove.

Unfortunately it is certain
That we have degenderized
'Chairman' and deglamorized
'Postman' into 'Postal person.'

But that's another story.
I flinch when PC clones
Are ruggedized, the telephones
Restructurized. I'm sorry!

Now I suppose that common words
Should show some flexibility,
But *every* noun's verbability
Is truly for the birds.

E.g., in basketball, to outquick
And body-up tend to centerize
The game and disillusionize
Us all — tend to make us sick.

Language is in transition,
Which not one of us denies,
But all this *verbing* flies
In the face of tradition.

**

Yawning

Yawning is
A universal thing,
Dogs and cats do it,
Birds and rats do it,
But the longest string

Of yawns,
According to statistics,
Was observed in a mass
Of students in a class
Of higher mathematics.

Babies have
Been known to yawn
About five minutes —
Exactly five minutes,
After they were born.

It was
First hypothesized
That yawning was a scream,
Oh, a very silent scream,
As the lungs were oxygenized.

But later,
Some say science saith,
After many tests,
Following other tests,
That yawns and breath

Were not
Connected, and concluded that
Yawns and stretching —
That morning stretching —
They wore a common hat.

Lions and
Tigers, nature has decreed,
When they're in a zoo —
Much confined in a zoo —
Yawn just before it's time to feed.

Contagion is
A quality of yawns:
So that when *you* yawn
I will also yawn —
One yawn another spawns!

Notes

PART I

PROLOGUE

Page 17 *A Book For All Seasons*. In the Envoy to *Underwoods* (1887), Robert Louis Stevenson wrote:

> 'Go, little book, and wish to all
> Flowers in the garden, meat in the hall.'

Ecclesiastes III, 1:

> 'To everything there is a season, and a time to every purpose under the heaven.'

Page 23 *Come, Cicely, Let Us See*. The idea here came from Ben Jonson's *Song To Celia* (1607):

> 'Come, my Celia, let us prove
> While we can, the sports of love:
> Time will not be ours forever.'

Page 24 *The Creative Mind*. These verses grew out of my reading of Bill Moyer's interview with Nobel prize winner, Murray Gell-Mann. Creative thinking is needed especially by the poet, the artist and the scientist. The stages are: (1) Saturation; (2) Incubation; (3) Illumination.

The scientist has a fourth stage: Verification. Gell-Mann said that the ability to think creatively can be taught and learned, but only to some extent. My belief is that everyone possesses a God-given gift or talent. One's duty is to develop and use that gift as much as possible.

Page 25 *Designs*. The American poet, Howard Nemerov, wrote:

> 'The altering eye alters all.'

I altered the image to read:

> 'Each man's eye designs the world
> Each man's mind creates.'

Page 26 *Harvest*. In Stanza 13 of Wordsworth's poem, *A Poet's Epitaph*:

> 'The harvest of a quiet eye.'

To this I supplied a different subject, Beauty.

> 'Beauty is the harvest of a quiet eye,
> A poem is to hold that harvest high.'

Page 30 *In Praise of Plagiarism*. In his Foreword to *Underwoods*, Robert Louis Stevenson wrote:

> 'Of all my verse, like not a single line;
> But like my title, for it is not mine,
> The title from a better man I stole;
> Ah, how much better, had I stol'n the whole.'

That better man was Ben Jonson. See Note on *Stolen*, below.

Page 31 Mi Casa Es Su Casa. One warm spring afternoon, as I was pumping gas at a gas station on San Pedro, I glanced up and saw, not far away, the sign of a restaurant, Su Casa. In San Antonio, Texas, Spanish is a second language. Su Casa set me off to write these verses.

Page 33 *Reluctant Night*. The association of darkness and grief is as old as poetry itself. We find the following memorable stanza in Carl Sandburg's *The People Will Live On* (1936):

> 'Who can live without hope?
> In the darkness with a great bundle of grief
> the people march.'

Page 35　*Somewhere.* Even Nonsense Verse needs ideas and images. Lewis Carroll is the best source. But my poem was suggested by the first lines of Rupert Brooke's *Heaven*:

> 'Somewhere, behind Space and Time,
> Is wetter water, slimier slime!'

Page 36　*Spending. To Olive* is perhaps the only poem by Lord Alfred Douglas that is remembered:

> 'I have been profligate of happiness
> And reckless of the world's hostility.'

Page 37　*Surprise.* In a letter to John Taylor (February 27, 1818), John Keats wrote:

> 'Poetry should surprise by a fine excess, and not by singularity. It should strike the reader as a wording of his own highest thoughts, and appear almost as a remembrance.'

Page 40　*Two Little Girls.* In the final stanza, Lexus is a car made by Toyota, whereas Infinity is made by Nissan.

PART II

NATURE

Page 46　*At Sundown.* In Book II, Line 420, of Homer's *Odyssey*:

> 'A favorable wind clear-eyed Athene sent,
> a brisk west wind that sang along the wine-dark sea.'

Page 48　*Day.* The image I use here — 'The vault of night' — was suggested by Robert Burns' poem, *Tam o'Shanter*, (1793):

> '...o' night's black arch.'

Page 49　*The Desert.* In the third stanza: Devil's Rope is barbed wire. Saguaros are large cactus plants, often as tall as trees (up to forty feet), with thick, spiny stems and white flowers – the State flower of

Arizona. Saguaros flourish in parts of Central America, in Arizona and along the Colorado River in southern California. When the spring rains fall, the desert blooms with color.

Page 54 *Gravity.* In his classic book, *A Brief History Of Time* (1988), page 73, Stephen Hawking writes:

'In this book, I have given special prominence to the laws that govern gravity, because it is gravity that shapes the large-scale structure of the universe, even though it is the weakest of the four categories of forces.'

The four categories of forces are: 1) gravitational force; 2) electromagnetic force; 3) the weak nuclear force; and 4) the strong nuclear force, which holds the protons and neutrons together in the nucleus of an atom.

On page 70, Hawking writes: 'Real gravitons make up what classical physicists call gravitational waves, which are very weak – and so difficult to detect that they have never yet been observed.'

For more on the subject of particle physics, see Note on *Nature's Irregularities*, below.

Page 55 *It Is Time.* In his oft-quoted poem, *Stopping by Woods on a Snowy Evening*, Robert Frost wrote:

'The woods are lovely, dark and deep.'

Page 57 *Like The First.* The hymn, 'Morning Has Broken,' may be found on page 145 of the 1989 edition of *The United Methodist Hymnal*:

'Morning has broken, like the first morning,
Blackbird has spoken, like the first bird.'

Page 60 *Nature.* In her poem, *Nature*, Emily Dickinson wrote:

'The pedigree of honey
Does not concern the bee.
A clover any time to him
Is aristocracy.'

Page 61 *Nature's Irregularities.* Two American physicists, Chen Ning Yang and Tsung-Dao Lee, received the Nobel Prize in 1957 for their work in particle physics. In 1969, the Nobel Prize for Physics went to Murray Gell-Mann, whose work was in the field of very small particles he called 'quarks'. He took the name from James Joyce: 'Three quarks for Muster Mark!'

See Stephen Hawking's *A Brief History of Time*. Hawking holds the Newtonian Chair as Lucasian Professor of Mathematics at Cambridge University, England. He is widely regarded as the most brilliant physicist since Einstein.

See Note on 'Gravity,' above.

Page 63 *Nature's Law*. The ideas and images here come from many sources. Walter Scott, in *Lady of the Lake*:

'The rose is fairest when 'tis budding new.'

John Dryden, in *Fables*:

'Art may err, but nature cannot miss.'

Page 67 *Russian Evening*. These verses are indebted to ideas and images from the article, 'Most Beloved', which appeared in the March 4, 1991, issue of *The New Yorker*. The author is Tatyana Tolstaya. The translator, Jamey Gambrell.

Page 71 *The Silent Seasons*. The American poet, Howard Nemerov, provided me with the idea for these verses. His phrase, *soft suddenness*, I converted to *sudden softness*. He also used the image, *the floor of summer*.

Page 77 *Thunder And Lightning*. *Macbeth*, Act I, Scene 1:

First Witch: 'Where shall we three meet again,
In thunder, lightning, or in rain?'

Page 79 *The Vagaries of Nature*. Robert Hughes, art critic for *Time*, puts forth the opinion that any object in a picture *may* be wrapped about by rays of light.

Page 81 *When the Trees Put on Their Joseph Coats*. Israel loved his young son Joseph more than all the others and made him a coat of many colours. The story may be found in the 37th chapter of *Genesis*.

Page 82 *Wide As A Dream*. Walter Scott wrote in Stanza 17 of Canto VI,
Lochinvar:

> 'Oh, what a tangled web we weave,
> When first we practise to deceive!'

Page 86 *The Winds of Spring*. Rudyard Kipling has a poem called *In
Springtime*:

> '...woodlands where the winds of Springtime
> range.'

PART III

TRAVEL

Page 92 *China Is Dark*. In the early morning hours of June 4, 1989, hope
died and fear was born on the killing field of Tiananmen
Square, as the protesting students were slaughtered by the thousands.
Later, Li Ping said to the Army troops, 'Thank you for your hard work.'
A river of blood flowed on that terrible day in Tiananmen Square. The
world will long remember!

Page 93 *The City At Night*. In her novel, *A Taste for Death*, P. D. James
writes:

> 'The city at night is a world patterned in light.'

Page 95 *English Journey*. Six years of my military career have been spent
in the British Isles. During World War II, I was Radar Officer
for the 492nd Bomb Group, stationed in the Midlands. I wrote a novel in
1944, and it was published by W. H. Allen & Company Ltd., with the title
We Always Come Back. The New York edition followed in late 1945.

From the fall of 1960 to the fall of 1964, I was the Assistant Operations
Officer of the 6950th Radio Group Mobile, stationed at RAF Chicksands,
ten miles from Bedford, forty miles from London and forty miles from
Cambridge. The four years at Chicksands resulted in a novel, *The
Commander*, published in 1985 by the Pentland Press. My six years in
England and Scotland provide much of the material in *English Journey*.

In 1987, I extracted lines and images from this long poem and wrote two short poems, which were published in Vol. VII, Number 2 of the *American Poetry Anthology*. The first I titled *English Journey*:

Low white stiles cross grey fences,
Waving seas of tawny barley.
Royston Road nicks Newmarket,
Horses gallop on the Downs,
Heads held high, nostrils all aquiver.
Chestnut trees shade the trails
Leading back to scattered barns.
Restless winds frighten birds.

Blowing clouds scud the sky,
Willows weep along the Cam.
Churches grow on tombstoned greens,
Arches finely etched in Norman towers,
Gleaming windows cut from amber rock.
The nave is dark and cool,
Music whispers from the organ loft.
Day is blessed with sudden sun.

Limestone slopes climb the
Gentle Cotswold hills.
Sheep glean the shining meadows,
Lambs leap in awkward gambol.
Silver streams — ducks a-waddling —
Tiny bridges built of stone,
Neat-thatched houses on a reedy river.
Trees with feather tops.

The second short poem was titled *Scotland*:

Carlisle and Dumfries lie along the roads
To Scotland's deepening dales.
Cotton clouds swing across the hanging valleys.
Rocky hills smeared with lichen —
Rusty orange and brilliant green.
Burnished sea of bracken,
Emerald streaked with hints of gold.
Purple heather hides the hillsides.

Now the day is opalescent with twilight,
The Castle gleams upon the hill.
Now the Firth reflects the dying rays.
Peace returns to Princes Street.
Now the darkness walks the Royal Mile.
Shadows rise from cooling stones
And shroud the Heart of Midlothian.
Night descends – quiet as ashes falling.

Page 102 *On The Way To Santa Fe*. My wife, Cicely, and I had occasion several times during 1980 to drive to Santa Fe, New Mexico. When you're driving in New Mexico, you are never out of sight of mountains. My artist sister, Mary Bonkemeyer, lived for a number of years in Santa Fe, known for its artists and art galleries, for the opera and for its ski slopes.

PART IV

MORALS AND METAPHYSICS

Page 110 *A Haunting Dream That Lingered*. In his poem, *A Dream Within A Dream*, Edgar Allan Poe wrote:

'All that we see or seem
Is but a dream within a dream.'

Page 111 *All*. In *My Own Epitaph*. John Gay wrote:

'Life is a jest, and all things show it.
I thought so once, but now I know it.'
Hence my final line: 'But often/All is jest.'

Page 120 *Awkward*. Mona Van Duyn, winner of the National Book Award in 1971, supplied this image:

'Awkward as a half-grown bird.'

Page 121 *Beauty*. In her poem, *Vignettes Overseas: Off Algiers*, Sara Teasdale demonstrates her alliterative powers in these two lines:

'When unexpected beauty burns
Like sudden sunlight on the sea.'

Page 123 *Beware.* In Line 1205 of *Iphigenia In Tauris*, Euripides wrote:

'Beware of gifts that emanate from Greece.'

Book II, Line 49 of Virgil's *Aeneid*:

'I fear the Greeks even when bringing gifts.'

Page 125 *Chaos.* As here used, the word 'chaos' has a special, or scientific, meaning, and refers to the state of matter (in physics), or to numbers (in mathematics).

Page 139 *Fear.* In Stanza 1 of *In The Wood of Finvara*, Arthur Symonds wrote:

'Life is a dream in the night, a fear among fears,
A naked runner lost in a storm of spears.'

Henry David Thoreau wrote in his *Journal*, September 7, 1851:

'Nothing is so much to be feared as fear.'

In one of his fireside chats, President Franklin Delano Roosevelt declared: 'The only thing we have to fear is fear itself.'

Page 140 *Fictionized.* Eavan Boland's poem, *Distances*, appeared in the February 19, 1990, issue of *The New Yorker*:

'A fine rain fictionizes distances.'

Page 141 *Fortune.* Little-known author, Winthrop Mackworth, wrote a small poem called *The Haunted Tree*:

'Dame fortune is a fickle gypsy
And always blind and often tipsy.'

Page 145 *Greed.* In his *Letter to Timothy*, Chapter III, Verse 3, St. Paul wrote:

'A bishop must then be . . . not given to wine,
no striker, not greedy of filthy lucre;
but patient, not a brawler, not covetous. . . .'

Page 146 *Happiness.* In Chapter 38 of Tolstoi's *What Shall We Do Then?* (1886):

> 'The happiness of men consists in life.
> And life is in labor.'

On page 399 of George Du Maurier's *Peter Ibbetson* (1891):

> 'Happiness is like time and space — we make and measure it ourselves.'

Volume II, Chapter 29, *The Life of Sir William Osler*:

> 'No man is really happy or safe without a hobby, and it makes precious little difference what the outside interest may be —'

Page 151 *History.* Leon Bloy, the French novelist, wrote:

> 'History unfurls as God's secret . . .
> History is also man's destiny, from which there is no abdication.'

John Elson wrote the Essay, 'Apocalypse Now', for *Time* magazine, February 11, 1991:

His opinion is that nobody really learns from History. Actually, each generation interprets History in the light of current knowledge and experience.

Page 152 *Home.* Lance Morrow wrote an Essay for *Time* magazine, December 24, 1990, 'Home Is The Bright Cave Under The Hat'. He suggests three ideas:

> The womb is the first home.
> Home is all the civilization that a child knows.
> Home is a place to run away from when the time comes.'

Page 153 *Hormones.* George F. Will is a thinking-man's writer, syndicated columnist and contributor to *Newsweek* magazine. He wrote:

> 'High school in the 1980s was a sea of faded denims and raging hormones.'

Page 158 *In Defense of Darwin.* In 1859, Charles Robert Darwin published his classic book, *The Origin of Species.* In Chapter 3, he wrote:

'I have called this principle, by which each slight variation, if useful, is preserved, by the term Natural Selection.'

The concept of a 'godly grammar' beneath the apparent chaos of the universe came from my reading of C.S. Lewis.

Page 160 *Inspiration.* In Chapter 24 of his *Life*, Thomas Alva Edison wrote:

'Genius is one per cent inspiration and ninety-nine per cent perspiration.'

Page 163 *The Judgment Day.* In his *Letters*, Franz Kafka wrote:

'Only our concept of Time makes it possible for us to speak of the Day of Judgment by that name; in reality it is a summary court in perpetual session.'

Page 165 *Laughter.* In *To a Skylark*, Stanza 18, Shelley wrote:

'Our sincerest laughter
With some pain is fraught.'

Page 166 *Laughter – 2.* In his *Dedicatory Ode*, Hilaire Belloc wrote:

'There is nothing worth the wear of winning
But laughter and the love of friends.'

Page 167 *Life.* John Updike, winner of two Pulitzer Prizes for fiction, is author of the line:

'A garden is a river flowing south.'

Page 168 *Lighter Than A Breath.* In the *Old Testament*, Verse 9 of the sixty-second Psalm:

'Surely men of low degree are vanity, and men of high degree are a lie: to be laid in the balance, they are altogether lighter than a breath.'

Page 170 *Love.* In *Hope Is Like a Harebell*, Christina Rossetti wrote:

'Hope is like a harebell trembling from its birth,
Love is like a rose the joy of all the earth.'

Page 172 *Miracles.* In his book, *Miracles*, C.S. Lewis, wrote:

'Nature, as we know it, is not the whole of reality, but only a part of it. Reality extends far beyond nature, and when that reality throws something new into nature, we say that a miracle has occurred. But once a miracle does occur, that new thing is accepted by nature and becomes a part of nature and is subject to all of nature's laws.'

My verses state that all of life, even the simplest of things, constitutes a miracle. This, of course, is a figure of speech. But I believe that figures of speech may enfold a fundamental truth.

Page 173 *Moderation.* Around 42 B.C., Theognis wrote:

'Be not too zealous, moderation is best in all things.'

In *Medea*, Euripides says:

'Moderation, the noblest gift of heaven.'

Plutarch advised:

'Moderation is best . . . avoid all extremes.'

Shakespeare, in *Troilus and Cressida*:

'Be moderate, be moderate.'

Montaigne, in his *Essays*, Book III, Chapter 13:

' . . . the most moderate measure (is) the most perfect.'

Page 175 *Money.* Pubilius Syrus wrote in *Maxim* 633:

'Money alone sets all the world in motion.'

In Book II of his *Satires*, the Roman poet, Horace, writes:

'Get place and wealth, if possible with grace,
If not, by any means get wealth and place.'

In Canto XI of *Don Juan*, Lord Byron wrote:

'Ready money is Aladdin's lamp.'

In his 1860 Essay on *Wealth*, Emerson said:

'The world is his who has money to go over it.'

Emerson also said: 'Money is...as beautiful as roses.'
The Apostle Paul wrote in his *Letter to Timothy*:

'The love of money is the root of all evil.'

This is often misquoted as, 'Money is the root of all evil.' Not
so. It's the *love* of money that is the root of all evil. That is, a
great deal of all evil, for evil has many roots.

Page 177 *Mystery*. In October, 1930, Einstein told an American audience
in his lecture, *What I Believe*:

'The most beautiful thing we can experience is the
mysterious.'

Mary Mapes Dodge, is her poem, *The Two Mysteries*, wrote:

'Life is a mystery as deep as ever death can be.
Yet, oh, how sweet it is to us, this life we live and
see.'

Page 180 *Niche Is In*. In *Powershift*, Alvin Toffler writes:

'Mass is out, niche is in.'

Page 181 *Now, Go, My Love*. See Note above on *Come, Cicely, Let Us
See*.

Page 186 *Paradoxes*. Lucy Larcom wrote one memorable poem, *Black in
Blue Sky*. Stanza 2 reads:

'There is light in shadow and shadow in light,
And black in the blue of sky.'

Page 187 *Paradoxes – 2*. The familiar proverb, 'History repeats itself',
suggested to me that 'History is prediction.'
An obscure poet named Winthrop Praed, wrote the line:

'Events are writ by History's pen.'

Page 188 *The Paradox of Vanity*. In *Ecclesiastes*, I, 2:

'Vanity of vanities; all is vanity.'

Page 191 *Pleasure*. In Canto IV, Stanza 178 of *Childe Harold's
Pilgrimage*, Byron writes:

'There is pleasure in the pathless woods,
There is rapture on the lonely shore.'

In Stanza 1 of the *Chorus* to *Atlanta in Calydon*, Swinburne
wrote:

'Pleasure, with pain for leaven.'

Robert Burns in Stanza 7 of *Tam o'Shanter*:

'But pleasures are like poppies spread,
You seize the flower, its bloom is shed.'

Page 192 *Power*. The British Prime Minister, William Pitt, wrote in his
January 9, 1770, speech, *Case of Wilkes*:

'Unlimited power is apt to corrupt the minds of those
who possess it.'

In his 1887 *Letter to Bishop Mandell Creighton*, Lord Acton
wrote:

'Power tends to corrupt. Absolute power corrupts
absolutely.'

Page 194 *Prosperity*. Act IV, Scene 3, Line 586 of Shakespeare's *The
Winter's Tale*:

'Prosperity's the very bond of love
Whose fresh complexion and whose heart together
Affliction alters.'

Francis Bacon in his Essay 'Of Adversity':

'Prosperity is not without many fears and distastes;
and adversity is not without comforts and hopes.'

Page 197 *Reality*. This short poem was first published in Vol. IV, No. 3 of
American Poetry Anthology (1985). The concept of childhood
as a time of innocence and magic is as old as poetry itself. Do not forget that
poetry is older than prose. On the other hand, the small child is extremely
selfish. Learning to share comes with long training, if, indeed, it comes at
all.

Page 199 *Riches, Fame and Pleasure.* In 1677, the philosopher Spinoza
published his *Tractatus de Intellectus Emendacione.* In Part I,
Section 3:

'The things which are esteemed as the greatest good of
all . . . (are) to wit, Riches, Fame and Pleasure.'

The Bible contains numerous references to riches (wealth),
fame and pleasure. Herewith only a few:

'Wealth maketh many friends.' *Proverbs*, XIX, 4.
'A good name is rather to be chosen than great riches.' *Ibid*,
XXII, 1.
'Riches certainly make themselves wings.' *Ibid*, XXIII, 5.
'Let us now praise famous men . . .' *Ecclesiastes*, XLIV, 1.

In *The Letters of Junius* (Identity unknown), LIX:

'The temple of fame is the shortest passage to riches
and preferment.'

Washington Irving's *The Sketch-Book, Westminster Abbey*
(*The Corner*):

'His (the author's) renown (fame) has been purchased, not by
deeds of violence and blood, but by the diligent dispensation of
pleasure.'

Philip Doddridge (circa 1750) wrote an *Epigram on His Family
Arms*:

'Live while you live, the epicure would say,
And seize the pleasures of the day . . .'

Samuel Pepys wrote in his *Diary*, March 10, 1666:

'The truth is, I do indulge myself a little the more in
pleasure, knowing that this is the proper age of my life to do
it . . . .'

Page 202 *Seeds.* As most everyone knows, when plants and flowers die,
they shed their seeds, which, in fertile ground, grow and live
again. The cycle of life and death and life goes on forever.

Page 203 *Silence*. Robert Louis Stevenson writes in *Truth of Intercourse*:

'The cruellest lies are often told in silence.'

In 1876, Samuel M. Hageman wrote the poem *Silence*:

'Every sound shall end in silence, but the silence never dies.'

A Swedish Inscription: 'Speech is silvern, Silence is golden.'

Page 208 *Think Your Way*. In *Something of Myself*, Kipling writes:

'When your Daemon is in charge, do not try to think consciously. Drift, wait and obey.'

Page 209 *Thoughts*. *Dialogues of Alfred North Whitehead* (1953), page 100:

'The vitality of thought is in adventure. *Ideas won't keep*. Something must be done about them. When the idea is new, its custodians have fervour, live for it, and, if need be, die for it.'

Page 210 *Three Things Most Needed Are*. Ella Higginson wrote a classic little poem, *Four-Leaf Clover*:

'One leaf is for hope, and one is for faith,
And one is for love, you know,
And God put another in for luck.'

Persian proverb: 'Luck is infatuated with the efficient.'

In *Distichs*, XV, John Hay wrote:

'True luck consists not in holding the best of the cards at the table;
Luckiest he who knows just when to rise and go home.'

Page 211 *Time*. The key source on *Time* is Stephen Hawking's classic book, *A Brief History of Time* (1988). One theory holds that time began when the Big Bang occurred. Hawking soars brilliantly across the vastness of space and time to unlock the secrets of the universe. Early philosophers held that Time was absolute. But Albert Einstein proved that space is curved and time is relative. The universe which Einstein observed had a finite beginning and, probably, would have an end.

Page 212 *The Tree of Life.* 'Taxonomy' is the laws and principles of classification, especially the classification of plants and animals according to their natural relationships.

Page 214 *Truth.* In Chapter 18, Verses 37–38 of the *Gospel of St. John*:

> 'Jesus said, To this end was I born, and for this cause came I into the world, that I should bear witness unto the truth. Everyone that is of the truth heareth my voice. Pilate said unto him, What is truth?'

Page 215 *Truth And Error.* William Cullen Bryant wrote in Stanza 9 of *The Battle-Field*:

> 'Truth, crushed to earth, shall rise again.'

Matthew, Chapter VI, Verse 28: 'Consider the lilies of the field, how they grow; they toil not, neither do they spin.'

Page 217 *Truth And Fiction.* Canto XIV, Stanza 101, *Don Juan*, by Lord Byron:

> ' 'Tis strange but true; for truth is always strange — Stranger than fiction.'

Page 219 *Truth Is No Stranger.* In his famous poem, *To The Rock That Will Be a Cornerstone*, Robinson Jeffers wrote:

> 'Lend me the stone strength of the past and I will lend you The wings of the future, for I have them.'

Page 221 *Variety.* In Book II, Line 606 of *The Timepiece*, by William Cooper:

> 'Variety's the very spice of life.'

Pubilius Syrus (*circa* 42 B.C.) wrote:

> 'No pleasure endures unseasoned by variety.'

Benjamin Disraeli, in Book V, Chapter 4, of *Vivian Grey*:

'Variety is the mother of enjoyment.'

Page 222 *War*. When I write that 'War is part/Of nature's master plan,' I
am mindful of the words of a hundred men and women the
world over. The Bible tells us that there 'will always be wars and rumors of
war.' Benito Mussolini, in *The Italian Encyclopedia*:

'War alone brings up to its highest tension all
human energy....'

Albert Einstein:

'As long as there are sovereign nations possessing
power, war is inevitable.'

In *War-Song*, John Davidson wrote:

'And blood in torrents pour
In vain — always in vain,
For war breeds war again.'

Page 229 *Windows*. From lift off to landing, space travel is a child of the
computer. With the aid of the computer, space engineers were
able to find that critical moment in time, that window, through which
space travellers must pass on their way back into the atmosphere and to
land.

Public houses in the British Isles sometimes

'Put lavender in the windows,
Ancient ballads on the wall.'

When I was stationed at RAF Chicksands, my wife and I lived
for nearly a year in the market town of Hitchin, near which
there were fields of lavender growing.

Page 230 *Wit*. Line 90, Act II, Scene 2 of *Hamlet*:

'Brevity is the soul of wit.'

Page 231 *Wonder*. In *The Descent of Man*, Darwin wrote:

'Man, the wonder and the glory of the universe.'

In *The Nigger of the Narcissus*, 1898, Joseph Conrad wrote:

'But the artist... speaks to our capacity for delight and wonder, to the sense of mystery surrounding our lives, to our sense of pity and beauty and pain.'

The Seven Wonders of the Ancient World were:

The Pyramids of Egypt; the Hanging Gardens of Semi-ramis, at Babylon; the Statue of Zeus or Jupiter by Phidias, at Olympia; the Temple of Artemis, or Diana, at Ephesus; the Mausoleum at Halicarnassus; the Colossus of Rhodes; and the Pharos, or Lighthouse, at Alexandria.

PART V

MISCELLANY

Page 235 *A Gemstone Calendar.* Garnet is a gemstone a deep red in color. Janus is a Roman deity who is looking both ways, having two faces. In mythology, Janus is said to have worn a red garnet gemstone.

Amethyst is a gemstone not so rare as the red garnet. It is violet or deep purple in color, like the depths of the sea. Captain Nemo is the hero of Jules Verne's *Twenty Thousand Leagues Under The Sea.*

From *Turkey in the Straw, Stanza 6*: 'Sugar in the gourd and honey in the horn.'

Page 239 *A List of Things That Are Blue.* New Mexico is famous for (among other things) its blue cornmeal.

Quilts have patches of blue.

Bluebonnets are the State flower of Texas. They flourish in great numbers in April, especially when the rains have come in February and March.

Page 240 *A List of Things That Are Soft.* Dandelions, when they go to seed, are so light and soft they blow away in a breath.

Page 250 *Horse Racing*. My advice in The Kentucky Derby (the greatest
two minutes in world sports) is to stay clear of the favorite,
who rarely wins The Race for the Roses. Bet instead the horse whose odds
lie 'twixt 3- and 10-1. This held up again in the 1991 Derby. The favorite
ran 10th. The winner, Strike the Gold, went off at 9-2, which is $4\frac{1}{2}$-to-1.

I've written two books on horse racing: *How To Make A Million At The
Track* (Contemporary Books, Inc., Chicago, 1977), and *The Big Win*
(Pentland Press, Edinburgh, Scotland, 1983).

At Ascot, of course, you don't bet bucks (dollars). At Ascot, you'll never
make a pound, or almost never!

Page 254 *Stolen*. See my note above on *In Praise of Plagiarism*. In
Democritus to the Reader, Richard Burton wrote:

'They lard their lean books with the fat of others' works.
We can say nothing but what hath been said. Our poets steal
from Homer.'

In Line 41 to The Prologue to *Eunuchus*, Terence writes:

'In fine, nothing is said now that has not been said before.' In
Ecclesiastes XII, 9: 'There is nothing new under the sun.'

Page 259 *Universal Questions*. In the June 3, 1991, issue of *The New
Yorker*, John Updike wrote, for the BOOKS section, an essay
titled, 'At the Hairy Edge of the Possible'. He reviewed Alan Lightman's
and Roberta Brawer's new book, *Origins: The Lives and Worlds of
Modern Cosmologists* (Harvard; $29.95) and he covered several other
books, such as Fred Hoyle's *The Intelligent Universe*, Marcia Bartusiak's
Thursday's Universe, W. T. Atkins' *The Creation*, and Steven Wineberg's
The First Three Minutes.

Alpha '1' may be viewed as the symbol for the gravitational
constant and the strong-interactions constant that holds atomic
nuclei together.

Omega is 'the ratio of observed average mass density in the
universe to the critical mass density needed to halt, eventually,
the universe's outward expansion.' This ratio should be '1' but
observers have found it to be 0.1. Cosmologists cannot explain
this discrepancy, even when 'dark matter' is put into the
equation.

Dark matter is unobservable except by deduction — from gravitational motions within galaxies.

'Singularity' may be defined as 'some character or quality of a person or thing by which it is distinguished from all others' (Webster). In cosmology the Big Bang is a Singularity, being absolutely unique. At the moment of the Big Bang, the density of matter was infinite, and the 'curvature of space-time' was infinite (Stephen Hawking, *A Brief History of Time*, page 46).

'Irregularity' means not regular.

In cosmology, 'Inflation' is 'the theory that within its first second the mysteriously born big-bang universe, initially compressed to infinite smallness, achieved, under the pressure of a momentarily reversed gravitational force, and on top of its normal, sustained expansion, an exponential inflation from one-trillionth the size of a proton to the dimensions of a soft ball, or even by some accounts, of a basketball.' (*The New Yorker*, page 105).

The astronomer-physicist Marc Davis states that cosmology is 'data-starved'. Cosmology *needs* 'good data'.

John Updike contends that there is no good theory of how planet Earth acquired such a large satellite as the moon. No one seems to know why the sun rotates so much slower than it theoretically should.

Cosmologist Edwin Turner says that it is incredibly curious that the sun and the moon appear to have about the same angular size in the sky.

For an explanation of cosmological symmetries and supersymmetry, see Hawking's *Brief History of Time*, page 77-8. On 'Strings' see pages 159–162

Updike states that the 'observer' is essential. We exist here simply because we are here. Our life would be impossible on Jupiter or Venus. The anthropic principle uses the argument that certain properties of the universe depend on the fact that without those properties we would not be here to observe them.

Page 262 *To Verbal-ize*. James K. Kilpatrick, who once lived and worked in Scrabble, Virginia, now lives in Charleston, S.C. In one of his columns published in the *San Antonio Express-News*, Kilpatrick lamented the modern tendency to make verbs and gerunds out of nouns. I have 'used' several of his examples.

About the Author

Paul Ader lives with his wife Cicely in San Antonio, Texas. He has enjoyed two careers — one military, the other literary — running concurrently. He holds a B.A. Degree in English from Duke University (1940) and a Master's Degree in American Literature from the University of North Carolina at Chapel Hill (1949).

His military career covered two periods, the first from 1942 to 1945, the second from 1951 to 1969, when he retired in the rank of Lieutenant Colonel. During his early service, in World War II, he served the Eighth Air Force, in England. In 1944, he wrote a novel, *We Always Come Back*, published in 1945 by W. H. Allen Company Ltd. (London). Two years later he published his second novel, *The Leaf Against the Sky* (1947 Crown Publishers, New York). Following three years of graduate study at the University of North Carolina, he was recalled to the U.S. Air Force, and served as an Intelligence Officer until 1969.

Working in civilian life, he published a treatise on handicapping thoroughbred horses, *How to Make a Million at the Track* (1977, Henry Regnery Company, Chigaco). This was followed by a novel, *The Big Win* (1984, Pentland Press Ltd., Edinburgh, Scotland). One year later, his fourth novel was published, *The Commander* (1985, Pentland Press Ltd.). Pentland Press is now publishing his first volume of poems, *Designs And Other Verses*.

One of his works in progress is a novel based on the experiences of two women eighteen-wheeler drivers, who entered this male-dominated profession in the late 1950s and early 1960s.